STUDY SKILLS WORKOUT

STUDY SKILLS WORKOUT

Susan Campbell Bartoletti

Elaine Slivinski Lisandrelli

GERALD McALLISTER, CONSULTANT

Scott, Foresman and Company

Glenview, Illinois

London

Good Year Books
are available for preschool through grade 12
and for every basic curriculum subject plus
many enrichment areas. For more Good
Year Books, contact your local bookseller or
educational dealer. For a complete catalog
with information about other Good Year
Books, please write:

Good Year Books
Department GYB
1900 East Lake Avenue
Glenview, Illinois 60025

Table of Contents

Introduction to the Study Skills Workout
Teacher Introduction   1

I. Learning Styles
Teacher Introduction   3
Student Introduction   5
  How Do You Learn Best?   6
  How Do You Prefer to Show What You Have Learned?   8

II. Establishing Good Conditions for Studying
Teacher Introduction   11
Student Introduction   13
  Environmental Controls—Physical   14
  Environmental Controls—Mental   15
  Time—If I Only Had Time   17
  Dennis's Daily Log   19
  Tools of the Trade   20

III. Goal Setting
Teacher Introduction   21
Student Introduction   23
  Setting Short-Term Goals   24
  Planning Intermediate Goals   25
  Planning Long-Range Goals   26
  Mental Practice   27
  Handling Setbacks   28

IV. Becoming an Active Learner
Teacher Introduction   29
Student Introduction   31
  Thinking Types   32
  Getting to Know Your Textbook   34
  A Common Sense Approach to Homework   36
  "Quotable Quotes"   37
  Help a Friend   38
  The Magic of "If"   39

V. A Training Program for Effective Notetaking
Teacher Introduction   41
Student Introduction   43
  Do You Hear What I Hear?   44
  Classroom Notes—Get the Signal   46
  Note This! (Part 1)   47
  Note This! (Part 2)   49
  Book Notes—Top Secret   51
  Book Notes—Outlining   52
  Neat Notes   56

VI. *Exercising Your Memory*
    Teacher Introduction   57
    Student Introduction   59
        Why Remember?   60
        How Do I Remember?   61
        Memory Codes   63
        Picture Yourself (Part 1)   64
        Picture Yourself (Part 2)   66
        Association: One Way to a Better Memory   67
        Schooling Your Memory   69

VII. *Developing Stronger Test-Taking Skills*
    Teacher Introduction   71
    Student Introduction   73
        Why Take a Test?   74
        Preparing for Tests—Push the Panic Button?   75
        How Do I Prepare?   76
        Before the Test   77
        During the Test   78
        Don't Forget to Fill In All the Blanks   79
        True or False   80
        A Multiple Choice   81
        A Perfect Match   82
        An Effective Essay (Part 1)   83
        An Effective Essay (Part 2)   84
        When the Test Is Over   86
        Record Your Grades   88

Appendix
    Charting Your Progress   89

Introduction to the Study Skills Workout

TEACHER INTRODUCTION

How many children enter the school arena tired, out-of-shape, and ill-prepared to meet the challenges of the classroom? How many teachers want to help and show their concern yet are not sure where to start? The *Study Skills Workout* was developed to help all content teachers understand the factors and processes which influence good study skills and to provide these teachers with a strategy for integrating these skills in their curricula.

WHAT ARE STUDY SKILLS?

Study skills are thinking skills—necessary skills which help students learn how to continue learning on their own and how to become independent learners. In fact, by teaching your students good study skills, you are also teaching them how to think more effectively. The development of good study skills has far more implications than just the accumulation of a set of favorable grades; students are learning not only **how** to learn on their own, but they are also learning life-long survival skills for success.

Study skills, however, should not be **added** to an already overburdened curriculum. Instead, study skills should be **integrated** into an already existing curriculum. Content teachers should plan their various curricula together and use the information, suggestions, and plans from the *Study Skills Workout* in order to integrate consistent, structured, and sequenced study skills in each content.

USING THIS BOOK TO TEACH STUDY SKILLS

The **WORKOUT** concentrates on virtually every aspect conducive to acquiring good learning habits. Rather than approach study skills as a mere subset of reading, the **WORKOUT** deals with learning—knowledge, habits, skills, attitudes, and ideas. The exercises in the **WORKOUT** break these objectives into smaller components and provide teachers with consistency, structure, and a sequence for teaching these areas to students.

Each chapter begins with a teacher introduction that provides necessary background information on the objectives to be covered. A student introduction follows, explaining the objectives for the chapter. Both the teacher and student introductions are very important because they explain **what** is going to be covered and **why.**

Each subsequent exercise page is divided into three parts:

A. The Warm Up prepares the student for the lesson. It introduces the objective for the exercise to the student and explains necessary background material such as concepts and/or definitions.

These are the topics covered in the *Study Skills Workout*:

Chapter	Teacher	Student
I	How to employ teaching techniques to accommodate different learning styles	How to identify individual learning styles and use those styles to enhance learning
II	How to create and maintain classroom atmosphere and discipline for effective teaching	How to exercise control over mental and physical environment for effective study
III	How to guide students in defining, setting, and achieving goals as well as practicing mental rehearsal	How to define, set, and work toward goals and how to handle setbacks
IV	How to foster students' critical thinking abilities and get them actively involved in learning	How to become actively engaged in the learning process and to think more effectively
V	How to enhance students' listening skills and to take effective notes	How to listen more effectively and take good notes
VI	How memory works and how it can be strengthened through a variety of techniques	How memory works, how it can be improved, and techniques for remembering
VII	How to help students prepare for tests, how to develop tests that foster critical thinking, and how to help students in the testing process	How to overcome test anxiety, how to prepare for tests, and how to take tests
		Appendix—How to keep track of progress

B. The Work Out provides additional information and application of the new skill.

C. The Cool Down summarizes the skill, encourages discussion, and extends learning. Here, the students are also encouraged to apply the skill in situations outside of the classroom.

ADAPTING THE *STUDY SKILLS WORKOUT* FOR YOUR CLASSROOM

Many "how to study" books just give information and only talk about becoming a more effective learner. This book, however, is not only concerned with the knowledge of studying but also provides activities which get the students actively involved in developing good habits and skills. The activities in the **WORKOUT** are designed to show students of all ability levels that they are not alone in the problems they encounter—there are many plans they can follow to solve their problems.

Because there are no tests, per se, many students will view the objectives with a heightened interest. The students should be aware that the skills they are going to learn will be tested by how much they can apply—and improve—in areas both in and beyond the classroom.

Their attitudes will be strongly influenced by how the material from this book is presented. First, read over the teacher introduction pages that accompany each section. They are very important because they provide the necessary background information on the objectives to be covered. It is imperative that you, as well as your students, understand what is going to be covered and why.

Introduce the topics for each section—note new concepts, define difficult words, and promote group discussions. Students need to realize that their peers are valuable resources and that they can learn from each other as well as from a textbook. Allow your students the opportunity to try out new ideas verbally before and during the written exercises. Be sure your pupils know what is expected of them. In some instances specific answers are required; however, most often their answers will be rather subjective. Students should be permitted to develop some of their own "Cool Down" activities to encourage extending their learning outside of the classroom. Also, they should be encouraged to apply their skills in situations that are not school-related.

You should feel free to add and/or delete concepts and exercises to make the work more compatible to the age and ability levels of your class. It may be feasible, especially with slow learners, to have the students do some exercises in small groups of three or four. At times brighter students might assist the slower ones with written assignments. Occasionally, some of the exercises can be done orally.

Repetition is also very important for optimal development of any new skill; reinforce the study skills concepts whenever possible. Encourage your students to use these skills daily so they become habit forming. Review the appropriate study skills just before your students need to use them—to prepare for a quiz or testing situation, to prepare for an athletic or other event, to do a reading or writing assignment, to take notes or gather information from outside sources—and continue reinforcing them throughout the school year. Integration of the skills in other areas is also important, and this application can provide many interesting discussions.

Variety and enrichment can be developed through oral readings and discussions—allow some students to read their Work Out and Cool Down assignments aloud, or they can give an oral presentation of what they did. Role playing can be exciting; students can take the parts of parents, teachers, and students; their characters can reflect model parents, teachers, coaches, and students, as well as some not-so-model ones. They can present the various viewpoints on the "whys" and "hows" of applying their new skills. You might want to have students create posters "advertising" a particular chapter. Encourage your pupils to discuss how the information and skills acquired from their **WORKOUT** helped them succeed in and out of school.

Interaction among students, parents, and teachers to promote good study habits should also be fostered. Parents can be kept up-to-date with newsletters and/or meetings. Many parents are interested in the skills developed in the **WORKOUT** and appreciate information related to the skills. Also, many parents want to know how they can help their children at home. You might want to take a few tips from the teacher introduction as part of a newsletter to parents. As mentioned earlier, teachers should plan their various curricula together for optimal integration of study skills and consistency of their development.

An emphasis on developing a structured and sequential approach to fostering good study skills can become a goal for administration, faculty, students, and parents. A school-wide commitment to the promotion and development of a study skills program will instill in students a respect for hard work, a sense of pride and self-worth, and lifelong learning skills.

Learning Styles

TEACHER INTRODUCTION

Throughout all stages of our lives, we continue to learn, acquire knowledge, and process information through our senses and our perceptions of our world. Our five senses—sight, sound, touch, taste, and smell—bring information about our world to our brain. Our brain then perceives this information and processes it to acquire knowledge by noting differences and similarities, drawing conclusions, making generalizations, predicting outcomes, relating old information to new, and making abstractions.

We also have preferred ways of acquiring new knowledge; some of us prefer to learn by watching, some prefer listening, some prefer doing, and others prefer combining these modalities. The ability to process information effectively depends largely upon our understanding how to best use our preferred modality strengths to circumvent our weaknesses. For example, if you know that you cannot remember directions by simply hearing them, then you must overcome that inability by either drawing a map or writing the directions down.

The ability to use strengths to circumvent weaknesses is a skill that students must develop in order to function and succeed not only in the classroom but also in the outside world. This section—as well as the rest of the *Study Skills Workout*—is intended to help students as well as teachers identify their learning strengths and use those assets to minimize their learning weaknesses.

Our classrooms are filled with students who have preferred learning styles:

The **visual** learner—
    learns by watching
    likes to read
    has a vivid imagination
    shows emotions facially
    usually has neat penmanship
    dresses neatly
    plans and outlines
    takes neat notes
    likes order and neatness

The **auditory** learner—
    learns by listening
    likes to discuss
    remembers by reciting

will move lips while reading silently
    likes quiet
    is distracted by outside noise
    displays emotion through intonation

The **kinesthetic/tactile** learner—
    learns by doing
    needs to be directly involved
    likes to move around during study
    appears impulsive
    shows emotion through actions
    uses hands when talking
    does not tend to order and neatness

Children who are able to learn using a combination of the above styles (a multisensory approach) have an advantage in the classroom.

The role of the teacher is to construct a positive and productive learning climate for the student. The most effective classrooms are the ones that give students the opportunity to operate in all channels—a multisensory approach to education. Although it is not always possible to meet all the needs of all your students, it is important to understand that your students learn in many different ways.

The teaching style of most teachers reflects how they (the teachers) learn best—their preferred modality. Teachers should not ignore their own strengths, but they should give their students the opportunity to learn using all modalities. When students are given the opportunity to use their preferred learning style, and when that learning is reinforced by drawing upon secondary learning styles, students (and teachers) are more likely to experience success.

Here are some suggestions for integrating a multisensory approach to learning in your classroom (the chapters in the *Study Skills Workout* that address these suggestions in detail are identified in parentheses):

1. Give your students the opportunity to "take in" knowledge using as many modes as possible. Mix and match from the following suggestions:

Visually:
    a. Use teacher-prepared outlines, overhead projectors, and the chalkboard (Chapter V).
    b. Use A.V. materials such as filmstrips, etc.

c. Point out textbook aids such as charts, illustrations, bold print, and italics.

d. Teach your students how to take good notes (Chapter V).

e. When lecturing, establish good eye contact, use facial expressions and hand movements to emphasize key ideas, and prepare outlines (Chapter V).

f. Teach students how to use printed resources effectively (table of contents, index, glossary, as well as reference books) (Chapter IV).

g. Show effective memory techniques (flash cards, etc.) that are visual (Chapter VI).

Auditorally

a. Read directions out loud. Check for understanding by asking several students to repeat the directions in their own words.

b. Use the lecture method. Limit distracting classroom noise and emphasize key ideas through words and intonation (Chapter V).

c. Conduct discussions.

d. Tape record lessons and stories.

e. Use prerecorded records and tapes.

f. Use a phonics or sound approach to attack new words and spellings.

g. Teach effective memory techniques which employ the sense of sound (Chapter VI).

Kinesthetic/Tactile

a. Integrate hands-on projects that permit students to be involved in what they are learning.

b. Use small group activities.

c. Have students trace new words they are learning.

d. Encourage writing, drawing, and sculpting.

e. Use tapes that accompany the text.

f. Present illustrated lectures.

2. After students have "taken in" or received new information, there are two typical modes of expressing what they have learned—speaking and/or writing. A third mode—the motor mode or kinesthetic/tactile approach—is often overlooked. When students have the opportunity to express their learning using a variety of all three expressive modes, they are functioning at higher levels of cognitive processing. Give your students the opportunity to respond and/or express what they have learned in a variety of modes:

Written

a. Report in a variety of modes—essays, journals, story-writing, posters, charts, etc.

b. Encourage them to react to readings, pictures, etc.

Oral

a. Allow students to express themselves orally. Encourage them to expand on their ideas. Give them verbal clues to draw out more detailed responses. Help them to express their ideas clearly.

b. Conduct debates and panel discussions.

c. Assign oral presentations (speeches, etc.).

d. Provide time for recitation (poetry, times tables, rules, formulas).

e. Encourage them to ask and answer questions requiring various levels of cognitive processing (Chapter IV).

Motor

a. Assign projects that involve making models, dioramas, illustrations, charts, graphs, posters, collages, etc.

b. Provide role-playing situations.

c. Let them take part in plays.

d. Provide essay type tests and other written work.

As children grow and develop, their learning styles reflect their growth and development. Consequently, their preferred modality may shift. Learning styles and understanding how to use those styles for effective learning have implications in virtually every aspect of acquiring lifelong skills for success. Refer to this chapter often as you and your students progress through the *Study Skills Workout*. Help your students to see that they are not alone in the problems they encounter and that there are many plans they can follow to solve their problems. Encourage them to put their learning style to work for them.

Teachers should instruct, assign outside work, and evaluate using as many of the modes as possible for all the students. When students use a variety of modes to interpret and process new information, they are actively engaging their minds in the learning process: they are learning how to think more effectively.

Teachers should also provide as many examples as possible to promote understanding. Students should be able to hear new information, see it, and whenever possible, experience it. Understanding **how** one learns best and how to exercise those strengths can provide the basis for your students' lifelong acquisition of new learning.

Learning Styles

STUDENT INTRODUCTION

What is the best way for you to learn?

Have you ever seen how babies learn about their world? They use their five senses (taste, touch, smell, sight, and sound) to bring information about their world to their brains. Babies see new colors and objects. They listen to sounds and try to copy the sounds. When they see something new, they pick it up and sometimes they try to smell and taste the object.

You still learn about your world in the same way—through your senses. But you have different ways of gathering information from your senses. Some people like to gather information by watching or reading. Other people like to gather information by listening. Still others like to gather information by doing things.

It is important for you to understand how you like to learn because you can put that style of learning to work for you. In this chapter you will examine the way you like to learn. Throughout this book you will have the opportunity to put your strengths to work for you and to transform your weaknesses into strengths. You can use your strengths to learn how to become a better student and to learn how to do your best both in and outside of school.

How Do You Learn Best?

WARM UP

You learn about your world through your five senses. Your senses gather information and send it to your brain. When learning something new, most people have one sense they rely on more than the others.

Which of your senses do you like to use most when you gather information? Do you like to **watch, listen,** or **do** something when you are learning something new? This can tell you what **type** of learner you might be. There are three basic types of learners:

1. The **visual** learner prefers to learn by watching or reading.
2. The **auditory** learner prefers to learn by listening.
3. The **kinesthetic** learner prefers to learn by doing something.

When you understand the type of learner you are, you can use your strengths to learn new information more quickly—both in and out of school.

WORK OUT

Read over the following questions. Then write down the letter of the answer that best describes you.

1. Which assignment would you prefer?
   a. to read a short story
   b. to give an oral report
   c. to make a project

2. Do you prefer to read stories with
   a. a lot of description?
   b. a lot of dialogue?
   c. a lot of action?

3. How would you wish to receive important information?
   a. in a letter
   b. over the phone
   c. in a code that you would have to translate

4. Look at one of your notebooks. Is it
   a. neat?
   b. passable?
   c. messy?

5. When you are trying to learn how to spell a new word, do you
   a. look at it carefully?
   b. spell it out loud a few times?
   c. write it a few times?

6. If you were putting a model together, would you
   a. read the directions carefully?
   b. discuss the directions with a parent or a friend?
   c. start to put the model together by trial and error?

7. Is your handwriting normally
   a. very neat?
   b. quite light?
   c. poorer toward the end of the assignment?

8. What do you remember best?
   a. faces
   b. names that you have heard
   c. things you have done

9. When you study, do you prefer
   a. a neat desk or table?
   b. absolute quiet?
   c. a comfortable area?

10. How do you react to new situations?
    a. look around but do not say much
    b. talk to another new person nearby
    c. try to do something to learn more about it

11. How would you create an ideal friend?
    a. imagine the personality and how the person would look
    b. make up a story in your head and then describe the person to your friends
    c. draw a picture of the new friend

12. During your free time at school, would you prefer to
    a. watch a filmstrip?
    b. listen to a speaker?
    c. do something (color, draw, clean the boards)?

13. Which club would you prefer to join?
    a. newspaper
    b. speech or debate
    c. drama

14. The teacher you seem to learn best from
    a. writes important information on the board.
    b. tells you the important information.
    c. has you work at your desk.

15. To study for a test, do you
    a. read your notes and textbook?
    b. have someone ask you questions?
    c. make up a sample test?

16. During your free time, do you enjoy
    a. reading a book?
    b. listening to music?
    c. doing something (playing a game) around the house?

COOL DOWN

Look over your answers. Count how many a's, b's, and c's you have.

a — means that you might have a visual learning style. That is, you prefer to learn by **watching**.

b — means that you might have an auditory learning style. You prefer to learn by **listening**.

c — means that you might have a kinesthetic learning style. You prefer to learn by **doing**.

If your scores are close in number, that means that you prefer to learn by using all of your senses.

You can use your style to help you learn. Throughout the chapters in the *Study Skills Workout* you will be learning many suggestions that you can use with your learning style. You might even learn **new** ways of making learning easier and more effective for you. The *Study Skills Workout* has many plans for many different types of learners. Discover how many more ways you can learn both in and out of school!

How Do You Prefer to Show What You Have Learned?

WARM UP

You already know that there are many ways your senses can send information to your brain. You also know that how much you learn depends on how you use the new information. Is the information old or new? Does the information have anything in common with information you already know? Is the information different? How can you use the information to help you learn?

How much you learn depends on the way you use the information. But, what is the best way for you to show what you know? How do you prefer to show what you have learned? Do you like to write down what you know? Do you like to discuss or tell what you have learned? Or, do you prefer to show what you have learned by making a project?

WORK OUT

Read the following questions. Then choose the answer that you feel describes the way you like to show what you know.

1. When you have free time, would you prefer to
   a. find someone to talk to?
   b. write someone a note?
   c. walk around or volunteer to work on a project?

2. If you had information to share with your class, would you
   a. give an oral report?
   b. put the information on the board or a handout?
   c. put on a skit?

3. For extra credit, would you prefer to
   a. make an oral presentation?
   b. do a research paper?
   c. make a project?

4. To solve a problem, would you
   a. talk about it with someone?
   b. write a note to someone?
   c. work it out by doing something physical, like running or playing basketball?

5. If you had to get in touch with someone you might like to have as a pen pal, would you like to
   a. make a tape-recorded message about yourself?
   b. write a letter about yourself?
   c. make a video at school that you could send?

6. Which special class would you prefer?
   a. a health class that has a lot of discussion
   b. a creative writing class
   c. a gym class

7. When you are explaining something that you have worked on, do you feel most comfortable by
   a. talking about the project?
   b. writing about the project?
   c. showing how to make the project?

8. If you were working in a group, which part of the assignment would you rather do?
   a. the oral report
   b. writing the report
   c. making the charts or posters to be used with the report

9. If you had to give someone directions, would you
   a. tell them?
   b. write them down?
   c. draw a map?

10. How can people tell what kind of a mood you are in?
    a. by the look on your face
    b. by your voice
    c. by what you do

11. What would be your favorite way of taking a test?
    a. out loud
    b. written test
    c. doing something (a project, etc.) to show what you have learned

12. If you were an "expert" on a particular hobby, would you
    a. tell people about it?
    b. write a story about it?
    c. build a display?

13. If you could pick any career you wanted in sports, would you
    a. be a commentator?
    b. write news stories?
    c. be a player?

COOL DOWN

Count the letters of your answers. Compare your scores with the information below:

a — You prefer to show what you know by **speaking.**
b — You prefer to show what you know by **writing.**
c — You prefer to show what you know by **doing.**

Use your scores to determine how you like to show what you have learned. Your learning style tells you what your strong points are and what areas you might need to work on. Even though you might seem to favor one style more than another, it is a good idea to be able to learn using all three styles. The more ways you are able to learn, the easier learning will become.

Concentrate on your strengths and use them to exercise your other styles. For instance, if you prefer to show what you know by writing, then use that style to help you when you have to give an oral report. As you go through school, you will have many opportunities to express yourself in different ways. Work hard at using your strong points to exercise your weaker areas.

From *Study Skills Workout,* Copyright © 1988 Scott, Foresman and Company.

Establishing Good Conditions for Studying

TEACHER INTRODUCTION

SUGGESTIONS FOR USING THIS CHAPTER

Although teachers have little control over the home lives of their students, it is still important for students to realize that they can try to control some factors of their lives and can learn to establish good conditions for studying. This section will cover the four major areas leading to an effective study environment:

1. Physical Environment
2. Mental Environment
3. Time Management
4. Study Equipment

Although the students' home learning climate is important, the classroom must be an effective climate as well. Before you begin to help your students examine ways in which they can improve their home learning climate, ask yourself if you are satisfied with your classroom climate. First, decide what your classroom needs are in terms of discipline and teaching strategies. Then, take a few minutes from your busy schedule to reflect on the questions posed in BOX A below. Ask yourself: Are your needs being met in the classroom?

BOX A: Questions for Reflection

1. Have you formulated a set of rules and procedures for your classroom?

2. Are your students clear on what these rules are?

3. Do you have a specific plan if a student chooses to disregard a rule?

4. Do you consistently follow through with your plan?

5. Do you stress the importance of learning?

6. Do you give attention to the way you use time in your classroom?

7. Do you have a system for the way you conduct your classes on a daily basis?

Now examine the following suggestions. Can you apply any of them to create a more effective classroom environment?

BOX B:
Suggestions for Creating a Positive Classroom Climate that Benefits Both You and Your Students

1. Manage your classroom in an orderly way. Even the most creative activities require careful planning and execution. You must express your expectations about assignments to your students. Be clear on the directions. You might even want to make up a checklist for students to follow while they are working. Good classroom management helps the lesson to proceed in an orderly manner. Students like order and a stable environment.

2. Clearly state rules. By clearly stating a rule, you are saying to your students, "This behavior is the appropriate behavior for my classroom." (What you deem appropriate is up to you. Do you want your students to raise their hands before they speak? Do you want them to enter a room quietly? Do you want them to bring the proper materials, etc.?) When the student exhibits the appropriate behavior you can reinforce it with praise.

3. Emphasize the positive. "Catch" students doing something right and let them know about it. Talk to them about their "right" behavior and tell them to keep up the good work. ("I like the way you handled that situation." "I like the way the majority of students are working quietly." "I like the way you read that passage with expression." "I like the way you raised your hand before you answered that question." "You did a fine job putting that problem on the board.") The behavior you choose to reinforce is the type of behavior that tends to be repeated.

4. Have a system for conducting class that both you and your students understand. Note that conducting an effective classroom means setting it up in three phases—the **warm up**, the **work out**, and the **cool down**.

WARM UP

A. Begin each class with a review of the previous day's material. You can review the material or you can call on students to do so. This technique is effective because it helps you to see if there are any problems you have to clear up before proceeding.

B. Explain the objective for the class period and tell your students how you plan to budget this class period. Explain how the new material fits in with what they have already learned.

C. Explain new or difficult concepts in advance; question the students to see if there are any background gaps that need to be filled in.

WORK OUT

A. Keep the students' minds actively engaged during the class. For optimal learning, students need to do something (i.e. take notes, respond to questions, etc.). If the class is centered around problems and seatwork, immediate reinforcement is necessary.

B. Keep in mind the various types of learners in your class (see Chapter I) and try to incorporate strategies to accommodate these students. Use the board or overhead during a lecture; incorporate projects into your curriculum; encourage students to write about what they have learned.

COOL DOWN

A. End each class with a summary and/or brief review of material covered during the class period.

B. "Publish" the fine efforts of your students. Use their work to create a bulletin board; encourage them to share their work in class; send home a paper with a good grade to be signed.

SUGGESTIONS FOR LEADING A DISCUSSION WITH STUDENTS BEFORE BEGINNING THIS SECTION

Begin this chapter with a discussion. Ask your students what sort of controls they can exercise over their study environments. Have the students share special techniques that work for them; have them discuss what sort of an environment they need in order to work effectively.

Talk to your students about their environment and why it is important to exercise control over factors that could make effective studying difficult. Loud music, TV programs in the background, poor lighting, cluttered desks or tables, phone calls, numerous interruptions, daydreaming, exhaustion, hunger, the inability to budget time, and the lack of the proper study tools are just some examples of negative factors to be discussed.

Tell your students that they do have some control over their physical and mental environment. Show them how you as a teacher try to control the environment in the classroom so that they can learn more readily. You can even share some of your own organizational techniques. Point out that making learning more enjoyable requires careful planning and management of time. Studying is still hard work, but as students learn tips on how to study well they can gain increased satisfaction from their hard work. Help them to see that they **can** exercise some control over their surroundings.

The activities in this section are geared to help make your students aware of their environment and realize they can make changes to help themselves. Stress that good organizational skills will not only benefit them now (the personal satisfaction of accomplishing tasks; earning better grades; having more time to do the things they like, etc.), but also these skills can bring them great rewards in their future personal and professional lives.

ESTABLISHING GOOD CONDITIONS FOR STUDYING

Establishing Good Conditions for Studying

STUDENT INTRODUCTION

Your environment (the conditions around you that affect your growth and development) is very important to you. Imagine how difficult it would be to study if you were stranded outdoors in the middle of a blizzard or if you were trapped in a cold, dark cave. Although these conditions are rather unlikely, there are other factors that you encounter each day that make study difficult.

These factors include TV programs or loud music blaring in the background, poor lighting, cluttered desks or tables, phone calls, and many other interruptions which create poor study habits. Daydreaming, exhaustion, hunger, an inability to budget your time, lack of proper study tools, and a lack of interest also prevent you from becoming a better student.

In this section of the **WORKOUT,** you will learn effective ways to control your physical and mental environment; you will receive helpful hints on learning how to manage your time; and you will learn how to get organized.

Although many suggestions will be presented so you can learn more efficiently, none of these activities will have any meaning unless it has **your** help. Yes, you are the most important person in this project. You have to be willing to make a very important contribution. You must be willing to have the proper attitude toward learning.

We can't promise you that learning will be all fun and excitement. **We *won't* promise that!!** Learning new material is often hard and time-consuming, but the rewards are great. Learning gives you the opportunity to use the talents you have to the fullest. Learning also gives you the opportunity to develop talents that you would like to have.

If you really dedicate yourself to becoming a better student, you will see that hard work is worth the time, the effort, and the struggle. If you begin to respect and appreciate hard work, you will have learned one of school's—and life's— most important lessons.

Environmental Controls—Physical

WARM UP

One step to becoming a strong student is learning to control your physical environment. Carefully examine the chart of physical do's and discover some of the conditions that help create a good study environment.

PHYSICAL DO'S

Do select a place in your home and make it your study space. Go to this place whenever you have homework.

Do have an uncluttered desk or table to work on.

Do gather all the materials you need **before** you begin to study.

Do have good lighting.

Do have a schedule on your desk and check off assignments as you complete them.

Do sit up straight in a straight chair (getting too comfortable while you study **does not** help you study).

Do make sure your study place is free from the distracting sounds of TV programs, loud music, and unnecessary conversations.

WORK OUT

Now that you've read some suggestions on how to create a good study environment, examine your present study conditions. Try to identify some of the problems you have. Then, tell what you can do to improve your study environment. Don't forget to look in PAULO'S PROBLEM BOX. You may see a problem of Paulo's that you are experiencing too, or you may have a problem he hasn't listed. If so, write your problem in the space provided. Then list a solution, or several solutions, that you think will help solve your problem.

EXAMPLE:

PROBLEM—My sister barges into my room when I am studying.

SOLUTION—I will shut the door and lock it when I am studying.

PAULO'S PROBLEM BOX
- lack of study space
- cluttered space
- poor lighting
- Study materials are scattered around.
- The TV distracts me.
- I have to answer the phone.
- I forget to do some assignments.

HERE'S MY PROBLEM

HERE'S MY SOLUTION

COOL DOWN

Select one of the problems you identified and try to solve it this week. First, think of all of the things you can do to help solve your problem. Then, list them on a clean sheet of paper. Next, discuss them with your parents, teachers, or friends. Select at least one solution and try to make it work. You will report back to the class in _____ days. Don't get discouraged if you have a setback. (Read about how to handle setbacks in Chapter III.)

ESTABLISHING GOOD CONDITIONS FOR STUDYING

WARM UP

Another step to becoming a good student is learning to control your mental environment. Carefully examine the chart of MENTAL DON'TS and discover some of the mental conditions that help create a good study environment.

MENTAL DON'TS

Don't study when you are tired.

Don't study when you are hungry.

Don't let your mind wander—instead, fight daydreaming.

Don't say "I'll put it off until tomorrow." (Start with your hardest task; then the rest will seem easy!)

Don't say, "I can't do it!" (Remember—you only learn what you want to!)

Don't say, "I never do anything right!" (Believe in yourself!)

Don't have an "I hate it" attitude toward homework. (If you try to make an unpleasant task more enjoyable, the task won't seem so bad. Try to find something good in everything you meet—including people.)

Don't say, "This is boring!"

WORK OUT

Now that you've read some of the pitfalls to avoid when studying, try to identify some of the problems you have. Don't forget to look in PILAR'S PROBLEM BOX on page 16 for problems you might share with her. Her difficulties might help you identify some of your problem areas. List some of your problems in the spaces provided. Come up with possible solutions. Write them down in the spaces provided.

EXAMPLE:

PROBLEM—I give up too easily.

SOLUTION—When I don't understand something, I will read it over again, look up words I don't know, or I will ask for help instead of giving up easily.

ESTABLISHING GOOD CONDITIONS FOR STUDYING   15

PILAR'S PROBLEM BOX

- I fall asleep when I try to study.
- I get distracted from my studies when I stop for snacks or to answer the telephone.
- I keep daydreaming.
- My stomach rumbles.
- I complain about my homework.
- If I don't understand something right away, I say it's too hard.
- I say that I will finish my work later, but I usually don't.

HERE'S MY PROBLEM

HERE'S MY SOLUTION

COOL DOWN

Select one of the problems you identified and try to solve it this week. Keep a chart or a journal and write at least one sentence each day telling if you were successful or unsuccessful. Don't become discouraged if your solution doesn't work at first. Keep trying. In _____ days we will have a group discussion on being able to control your mental environment. At that time you may want to share your feelings with the class.

ESTABLISHING GOOD CONDITIONS FOR STUDYING

WARM UP

It is often said that if you need something done, ask a busy person because the busy person knows how to budget time and get things done. Would you like to know how to make time to get your assignments done and still have plenty of time for yourself? Schedules can be your answer. You should write down **what** you have to study and when you are going to complete the work. Remember—people who have made our world a better place are people who have used their time wisely.

ANNIE'S ASSIGNMENT CHART

1. History. Read pp. 146-151 and take notes.
2. Spelling. Study first five words and write them 5x.
3. English. Do Ex. 10, 11, 12 on pp. 96-98.
4. Math. Do p. 25, problems 10, 20, 22, 23, and 26.
5. Science. Learn rules on p. 56.
6. Reading. No homework!! **Remember to bring in photos of Arizona to show Mr. Hartzell.

ANNIE'S TIME CHART

3:00-4:00 spend time with Amy
4:00-4:30 relax/have a snack
4:30-5:15 do history
5:15-5:30 help Mom with supper
5:30-6:00 eat supper
6:00-6:30 do English
6:30-7:00 relax/find photos
7:00-7:30 do math
7:30-7:45 do spelling
7:45-8:00 phone call to Maria
8:00-8:30 TV and snack
8:30-9:00 do science
9:00-9:15 read new book
9:15-9:30 get ready for bed
9:30—bedtime

WORK OUT

Examine ANNIE'S ASSIGNMENT CHART and her TIME CHART. Notice how she lists all of her assignments. Pay close attention to the way she budgets her time between school work and other activities and responsibilities.

Now fill in the blank assignment chart on page 18 with your own assignments. First, decide what your assignments are, what your responsibilities are at home, and the times that correspond with your schedule. Then, plan your schedule. Fill in the blank time chart with your own time schedule, assignments, and responsibilities.

Follow your chart for today. As you complete each assignment, check it off or cross it out lightly on your chart. Yes, even the "relax" section! At the end of the day you can be proud of all you have accomplished. Try to follow the chart as faithfully as you can, but an emergency may arise. If it does, deal with it and then rearrange your schedule accordingly.

COOL DOWN

Make an assignment chart and a time chart for _____ days. Stick to it. Eventually, keeping track of your assignments and the way you spend your time becomes a form of habit—a good habit!

ESTABLISHING GOOD CONDITIONS FOR STUDYING

ASSIGNMENT CHART

TIME CHART

ESTABLISHING GOOD CONDITIONS FOR STUDYING

WARM UP

There are many different ways to keep track of time. A daily log in which you keep track of every half hour you spend may be an effective way for you. This type of log also helps you see how much time can be wasted.

First, examine DENNIS'S DAILY LOG. Then, make a copy of his time log, but fill in your own information for tomorrow's date. Try to be as accurate and honest as possible. This type of schedule is especially good to follow at the beginning of each school year when you are trying to become familiar with your new class schedule.

WORK OUT

Dennis does not like to fritter his time away so he keeps track of **everything** he does. Although his friends laugh, his system works for him and he doesn't mind what they think. Will his system work for you? Why not give it a try?

COOL DOWN

Look over your daily log. Total up the time you spent in classes, the time you spent relaxing, the time you spent studying, and the time you wasted. Are there any ways you can prevent yourself from wasting time?

DENNIS'S DAILY LOG

Time	Activity	Time	Activity
6:00- 6:30	Get ready for school	2:00- 2:30	Reading
6:30- 7:00	Eat breakfast	2:30- 3:00	Library **Get research done on volcanos (Science)
7:00- 7:30	Review notes for test		
7:30- 8:00	Ride to school	3:00- 3:30	Ride home
8:00- 8:30	Wait for classes to begin—organize notes and books	3:30- 4:00	Relax—listen to radio
		4:00- 4:30	Chores
8:30- 9:00	English class	4:30- 5:00	Chores
9:00- 9:30	English class	5:00- 5:30	Supper
9:30-10:00	Study hall—do English homework	5:30- 6:00	Basketball practice
		6:00- 6:30	Basketball practice
10:00-10:30	Shop class	6:30- 7:00	Shower and relax
10:30-11:00	Science class	7:00- 7:30	Do science—Chapter 2
11:00-11:30	Science class	7:30- 8:00	Do math—problems on p.95
11:30-12:00	Lunch	8:00- 8:30	Read newspaper and talk on phone
12:00-12:30	Math		
12:30- 1:00	Math	8:30- 9:00	Watch TV
1:00- 1:30	Social studies **Do social studies homework (p.67, Ex. 12, 13, 14) in study hall tomorrow	9:00- 9:30	Watch TV
		9:30-10:00	Read
		10:00	Bedtime
1:30- 2:00	Social studies		

Tools of the Trade

WARM UP

When carpenters go to install kitchen cabinets, they come prepared with their tools. When plumbers arrive to fix leaky faucets, they have their tool boxes ready. When trained mechanics attempt to repair cars, they have the proper tools at their sides.

Do you have the proper tools when you study? If the answer is ''yes,'' then you will be ready for an uninterrupted study session. If not, you may waste hours each week looking for the tools you need.

WORK OUT

Examine the tool box below and circle the names of the study ''tools'' that will help a student get organized.

COOL DOWN

Make a list of the items you need on or nearby your study desk or table. Gather as many of the items as you can. Make them an important part of your study time.

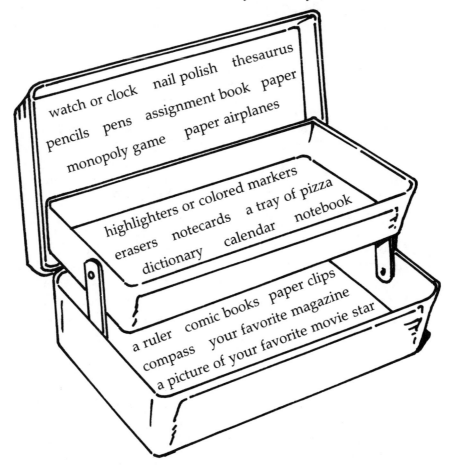

watch or clock   nail polish   thesaurus
pencils   pens   assignment book   paper
monopoly game   paper airplanes

highlighters or colored markers
erasers   notecards   a tray of pizza
dictionary   calendar   notebook

a ruler   comic books   paper clips
compass   your favorite magazine
a picture of your favorite movie star

Answers: watch or clock, assignment book, paper, pencils, pens, dictionary, eraser, paper clips, notecards, thesaurus, colored markers or highlighter pens, calendar, ruler, compass, and notebook.

Goal Setting

TEACHER INTRODUCTION

SUGGESTIONS FOR USING THIS CHAPTER

Most students do not actually plan to fail, but they experience failure because they do not plan adequately for success. If students are to be successful, they must make goals and work to achieve them.

If your students' progress is not as good as could be expected, it is because they need to plan better. Children—like many adults—need to have an **action** plan for success. They need to have a positive purpose; they need to set clearly defined goals and know how to achieve them.

In today's world the need for positive goals is especially necessary. People, both young and old, who have set clearly defined, positive goals and who strive to reach those goals tend to work and react to responsibility in a positive way. Goal-oriented children are better prepared for becoming mature, independent adults who recognize and accept responsibility, contribute to society, and provide for themselves and their families.

Most students who underachieve have poor study habits and/or lack motivation. When your pupils master the study skills in this book and become highly motivated, they will be well on their way to becoming higher achievers. Students who have specific goals are people who know what they want, why they want it, and how to get it; their goals are the engines that power their lives.

Effective teachers instruct, discipline (demand achievement), and motivate their students. You can aid your students by being goal-oriented yourself. You, as a role model, must reinforce and give positive feedback on your students' goals, and you must be explicit about your own objectives and expectations for the class (see Chapter II). If you want terrific results, you must have terrific goals. Hazy goals result in hazy results.

Goals, like habits, are learned behavior. Teachers can help their students turn goals into learned behavior by assisting them in setting clearly defined goals and working to reach them. As mentioned in the general introduction to the *Study Skills Workout*, taking the time for class discussion is important for the development of study skills. The activities in this section are designed to promote the discussion process. Make sure your students know what goals and dreams are. Encourage them to develop specific, sensory-rich, incremental goals. An incremental (step-by-step) approach to goal setting builds confidence; each small success leads to more successes. Sometimes, if students try to take a giant leap (for instance, going from a 52% to a 95%), they may fail, become frustrated, then give up. (See page 28, "Handling Setbacks.") It is important to set reachable goals.

Stress that goal setting is a process, and that goals can and should be adjusted from time to time. Success is not an ultimate destination of any sort. Rather, success is a continuing process of individual changes, accomplishments, and a sense of fulfillment. The most important facet of goal achieving is the change that occurs in the individuals—the persons they become as they travel toward their goals. They develop into high achievers who learn, conquer fears, and control stress. They become more responsible, inner-directed, and creative.

Successful people (winners, high achievers) have game plans and programs that are clearly defined and to which they refer constantly. The reason that most people never reach their goals is that they never really took the time to set specific, written goals in the first place. They fail by default. People who fail to plan, plan to fail.

Goal setting is extremely important; work hard with your students on this aspect of their lives.

SUGGESTIONS FOR DISCUSSION

The following are topics and/or questions that can be used with your students to help them think more deeply about setting goals:

1. The "Law of Harvest"—What you sow, you reap. If you think in negative terms, you will get negative results. If you think in positive terms, you will get positive results.

2. Dreams are lofty goals. Many famous people attained goals that began with a dream. Discuss some of these famous people and their dreams: Martin Luther King, Jr., John F. Kennedy, the Wright brothers, etc. Encourage your students to discuss some of their dreams and their plans for achieving them. Take a few minutes to think

---

about your own dreams and goals. Think big, work hard, and have a dream!

3. Only a small percentage of people (3-5 percent) actually consider themselves successful or are believed to be a success by others. What do goals have to do with this small number?

4. Think about what areas you consider to be successful about yourself. What are you good at? These are the areas that you have successfully developed. What other areas would you like to develop more?

5. Self-talk is our thinking; we are constantly talking to ourselves (at a rate of about 1000 words per minute!). Since we do talk to ourselves (i.e. think), shouldn't our thoughts be positive?

6.

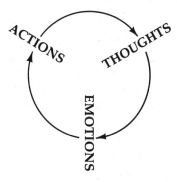

The **TEA** concept—When you have positive thoughts, you then have positive emotions (you feel good) and you have positive actions (you do ''good'' things). If you have negative thoughts, then negative emotions and actions will follow. Make the **positive** your cup of **TEA!**

7. You become what you think about! Think about your goals in a positive manner. If you control your thoughts, you control your life. What will happen if you think about failing?

8. Mental rehearsal—Practice **within** when **without.** That is, practice your goal mentally—go through all the steps and actions in your mind that are necessary for reaching your goal—when you cannot practice your goal physically (see page 27). You can practice reaching your goals mentally or in your imagination. Picture yourself in the process of getting there. Imagine the sights, sounds, even the smells of victory. Create all the necessary details in your imagination. This is a technique many famous athletes use to prepare before the ''big event.''

9. The **CBA** concept—Conceive, Believe, Achieve! When you think about a goal, and firmly believe that you can reach it, you will!

10. Responsibility—You are responsible (accountable) for your behavior, for your successes, and your failures. You are the ''Captain of Your Ship''; you cannot blame other people or fate for your state in life. Discuss this idea with your students. So many times students want to blame someone else for their misfortunes. A large factor in maturing is the ability to be accountable for their behavior, successes, and failures. Encourage them to analyze (see ''Handling Setbacks'' on page 28) their setbacks and decide on an appropriate action plan. If something is wrong, do something about it—doing beats stewing!

Goal Setting

STUDENT INTRODUCTION

Do you **plan** to fail?

Of course not! But if you don't set goals for yourself, if you **fail** to plan—then you might experience failure.

If you are not making as much progress as you would like, you need to learn how to **plan** better. You need to have a **positive** purpose. You need to learn how to set positive goals, how to go after those goals, how to think for success, and how to handle setbacks.

You already know that good study skills prepare you to continue learning on your own, long after you have left school. Goal setting is also a very important skill that you will continue to do after you have left school. Students who set clearly defined goals—students who know what goals they want, why they want their goals, and how to get their goals—are more prepared to become mature adults.

Think of clearly defined goals as an action plan for success. In order to be a winner, you must **make** it happen. Only **losers** let it happen. Think about the types of goals that are important to you. Is it success in school? Is it improving in a sport or hobby? How about success in an after school job? Would you like to become class president? Do you want to get along better with a friend or family member?

After you have decided what is important to you, write it down on a 3 × 5 index card. Make sure your goal is specific—for instance, success in school might mean doing better in math class or doing your homework regularly. Next, write down **why** you want your goal. You should be able to give two or three reasons. Finally, tape your goal to a spot that can be easily seen, like in a notebook, on a refrigerator at home, or even on your bedroom mirror. Be sure to read your goals at least twice a day. Goals should be a constant reminder of what you want and what you are working for.

Remember to pick goals that you can get excited about—exciting goals are the best goals. Everyone needs to feel the desire to succeed, but you must keep in mind that your beginning goals need to be reachable. Have you ever heard someone decide to lose ten pounds in a week? Or, have you ever seen someone begin an exercise program by trying to run five miles the first time out? Do these people stick to their plans? Why not? What do they need to do?

If you start with little successes, you will build your confidence and you will learn how to train yourself.

Setting Short-Term Goals

WARM UP

The following pages will explain the three basic types of goals: short-term, intermediate, and long-range goals.

Short-term goals are those that can be accomplished in a short period of time, usually ranging from a few days to a few weeks. Your goals can be related to school, family, or even personal goals that you have for yourself. Here are a few examples of short-term goals:

EXAMPLE 1—Erin wants to improve the number of sit-ups that she can do in gym class. So, every night she practices. She tries to do at least twenty-five in one minute and works on improving her score a little at a time.

EXAMPLE 2—Nicholas has to learn all the presidents in order. He knows it is hard to try to learn them all at once, so every night he learns five. Then, he reviews the ones from the previous night in addition to the new names he has learned.

EXAMPLE 3—Missy wants to save her allowance to buy a special birthday present for her brother. She knows it will take a while to save the amount of money she needs. So, Missy plans to save a little bit each day that she earns from her chores.

Each night that Erin, Nicholas, and Missy accomplish their goals, they make a mark on a calendar or in a notebook so that they can see their successes.

WORK OUT

Plan a short-term goal that you can accomplish within a week. Follow the steps listed below:

1. Decide on a specific goal (either academic, family, social, career, hobby, or sport). Keep in mind that you will use this goal for the next two goal exercises.

2. Write your goal down on a 3×5 index card.

3. Write the reasons why you want your goal.

4. Write down the steps you are going to take to achieve your goal. (Are you going to practice every night? Are you going to pay closer attention in class? etc.)

5. Carry your goal around with you or tape it where it can be easily seen. Be sure to read it at least twice a day.

6. Mark down each day that you work toward your goal on a calendar.

COOL DOWN

After you have reached your first short-term goal, make new ones. Just remember to work at maintaining each accomplished goal as it is reached. If, however, you did not do as well as you wanted to, don't give up. Try to figure out why. You might even have to readjust your steps.

SHORT-TERM GOAL

My short-term goal is _____

The reason(s) I want this goal is/are _____

What I have to do to get my goal _____

GOAL SETTING

Planning Intermediate Goals

WARM UP

Nothing great is ever accomplished by accident. If you want to accomplish something great, you must have an action plan based on clearly defined goals.

Intermediate goals come from short-term goals that work. Intermediate goals can be reached in a few months' time or less. Here are examples of intermediate goals:

EXAMPLE 1—Erin has accomplished her short-term goal of practicing her sit-ups every night. Now she wants to make an intermediate goal: Erin wants to be able to do forty sit-ups in one minute. Erin continues to practice every night by trying to improve a little bit at a time.

EXAMPLE 2—Nicholas has practiced his list of presidents every night, and he has met his goal! By the time the history test came around, Nicholas remembered every one and did very well on the test.

EXAMPLE 3—By doing her chores each day, Missy earned her allowance at the end of each week. She was able to save half of her allowance each week to put toward her brother's birthday present.

Success doesn't just happen. It is the result of planning and working at short-term goals. It is the result of making sure you accomplished your short-term goal every night.

WORK OUT

Plan an intermediate goal that you can accomplish within a few months' time. Follow the steps listed below:

1. Decide on an intermediate goal based on your earlier short-term goal.

2. Write your goal down on a 3×5 index card.

3. Write the reasons why you want your goal.

4. Write down the steps you are going to take to get your goal. (Are you going to practice every night? Are you going to pay closer attention in class? etc.)

5. Carry your goal around with you or tape it where it can be easily seen. Be sure to read it at least twice a day.

6. Mark down each day that you work toward your goal on a calendar.

COOL DOWN

After you accomplish this goal, make new ones. Just remember to maintain each success as you work toward new goals. Keep in mind that if you do not do as well as you had hoped, don't give up. Try to figure out what went wrong and readjust the steps in your plan.

INTERMEDIATE GOAL

My intermediate goal is _____

The reason(s) I want this goal is/are _____

What I have to do to get my goal _____

Planning Long-Range Goals

WARM UP

Long-range goals are goals that take from a year to a lifetime to accomplish. These goals usually mean that your short-term and intermediate goals are now **habits**—you are used to doing the necessary steps. You have trained yourself to accomplish what you want and you know how to get it. Congratulations!

Here are some examples of long-range goals:

EXAMPLE 1—Remember Erin, the girl who wanted to be able to do more sit-ups? She made a long-range goal of earning the Presidential Physical Fitness Award that her school gives out. By practicing each night and working hard, Erin was able to earn the award.

EXAMPLE 2—Nicholas not only did well on the history test that he had learned the names of the presidents for, but he also gained something far more important. Nicholas worked hard at improving his study skills. Nicholas learned how to study by preparing a little bit at a time for tests.

EXAMPLE 3—Missy worked hard at her chores every day so that she would earn enough allowance to buy her brother a birthday present. She saved half of her allowance to put toward his gift. Her long-range goal was successful! Not only was Missy able to buy her brother a present, but she also had some money left over—and she treated herself to a book she had wanted for a long time.

Erin, Nicholas, and Missy worked hard every night. Finally, their hard work paid off, and they reached their long-term goals. But something even more important was learned—new habits that would continue to benefit them.

WORK OUT

Plan a long-range goal that you hope to accomplish within a year. Follow the steps listed below:

1. Decide on a long-range goal based on your earlier short-term and intermediate goals.

2. Write your goal down on a 3×5 index card.

3. Write the reasons why you want your goal.

4. Write down the steps you are going to take to get your goal. (Are you going to practice every night? Are you going to pay closer attention in class? etc.)

5. Carry your goal around with you or tape it where it can be easily seen. Be sure to read it at least twice a day.

6. Mark down each day that you work toward your goal on a calendar.

COOL DOWN

Remember that you can do great things when you have enough reasons for doing them. Decide why you like to accomplish your goals. Is it the satisfaction it gives you? Do you like competition? Or do you have other reasons? Consider ''rewarding'' yourself each time you succeed at a goal. Maybe you'd like to break open the piggy bank or even just give yourself a night off!

LONG-RANGE GOAL

My long-range goal is _____

The reason(s) I want this goal is/are _____

What I have to do to get my goal _____

WARM UP

In life, people have to expect the best and look at the world around them in a positive way. Successful people have positive thoughts and positive goals. What you think and what you say to yourself (and it is estimated that people talk to themselves at a rate of about 1000 words per minute!) are important factors. Your thoughts determine how you feel about yourself and what kind of goals you work for.

You need to focus your energies on positive thoughts. Negative thoughts only drain your energies and emotions, and they make you feel tired and not very good about yourself. Positive thoughts, on the other hand, tend to energize your emotions. You feel good, you feel strong, and you do good things.

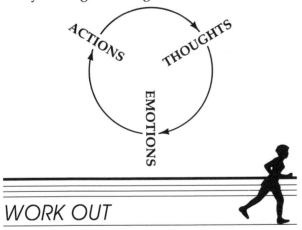

WORK OUT

Winners know that imagination rules the world. They know how important it is to train their minds as well as their bodies. Winners know how to practice mentally. You, too, can learn to practice mentally. Then, you will understand the power of your imagination. Try out the following mental activities.

MENTAL ACTIVITY #1

Think positively! Concentrate on the good things that happen each day and talk about these highlights with your family and friends or reflect upon them before you fall asleep at night.

Consider that not all goals have to be self-centered. You might want to consider helping other people as a goal. Use the following questions to frame your thinking:

1. What good happened today?

2. Did I learn anything new today (school-related or otherwise)?

3. Did anyone do anything that made me feel special today?

4. Did I do anything to help anyone else today?

5. Did I work toward any of my goals today?

MENTAL ACTIVITY #2

Each day when you read over your goals, you should imagine yourself reaching them. Read the following steps carefully. Then, use the steps to effectively practice **mental rehearsal.**

1. Close your eyes and get relaxed.

2. Imagine the goal you are working for. Picture, in detail, each step that you must take to get your goal.

3. How will you feel when you finally accomplish your goal?

4. Talk positively to yourself. Instead of saying, ''I think I can, I think I can...,'' say ''I know I can, I know I can....''

5. Believe in yourself. Remind yourself that you deserve your goal. You are important enough to earn success.

COOL DOWN

Mental practice has a ''domino'' effect: the more it is exercised, the easier it is to practice. Why waste time and energy on negative actions? With a little practice, encouragement, and consistency, mental practice can turn negative thoughts into positive purposes. Remember—you're only as smart as you think!

WARM UP

If you fail to reach a particular goal, does that mean you should give up? Does a setback in an action plan mean that success is not possible?

Of course not! If such a setback does occur, concentrate on what you are doing right rather than on whatever has gone wrong. Think about how you can learn from the setback. Remember that the future does not just get better by hoping. It does get better by planning and doing.

WORK OUT

Here are some suggestions for handling setbacks and disappointments.

1. Try not to enlarge the problem by giving up or reacting negatively to it (for example, ''getting even'' or feeling sorry for yourself). Remember that positive thinking will result in positive results.

2. Examine the setback closely. Is it really interfering with one of your goals? If the setback is a result of another person's behavior (for instance, if your coach chews you out at practice), does it really keep you from accomplishing your goal? Not really—not if you really want to earn your goal. Remember that you cannot control another person's thoughts or behavior. Let the other person keep his or her own negative behavior. You're too busy thinking positively!

3. If the setback is interfering with your goal, make a new action plan. Read over your list of goals again and your reasons for wanting your goals. Then, make adjustments if they are necessary. Finally, try harder—redouble your energies! Setbacks are only **temporary** inconveniences, but something positive can still result.

COOL DOWN

Here is a list of actual events from the life of a man who worked very hard but still met with failure. See if you can guess who he was!

1818—His mother died when he was nine years old.

1831—He lost his clerk job when the business failed.

1832—He was defeated when he ran for state legislature.

1835—His business partnership failed, leaving him $1100 in debt.

1836—He fell in love with a girl; she rejected his marriage proposal.

1843 & 1844—He lost the nomination to Congress both years.

1850—His second-born son died.

1858—He was defeated when he ran for the Senate.

1861—His third-born son died.

Answer: Abraham Lincoln

Becoming an Active Learner

TEACHER INTRODUCTION

SUGGESTIONS FOR USING THIS CHAPTER

One of our goals as teachers is to help our students become active, independent learners. Research has continually shown that **passive** learning is minimal learning. Students need to be **actively** engaged in the learning process: they need to think effectively on a variety of cognitive levels, they need to participate in class and ask questions, and they need to know how to become **active** learners.

Successful students are active students. This chapter of the **WORKOUT** presents various activities to make students aware that they can be actively involved in the learning process: The exercises in this chapter focus on thinking skills, textbook appreciation, homework tips, and the characteristics of the active learner. As you work on the exercises together, help your students develop the proper attitude toward "taking charge" of their learning situation. In your discussions with your students, help them to see that there will be rewards for being active learners: School-work will be less of a burden, grades will improve, and learning will be challenging and exciting. Their self-image will improve as they begin to feel satisfaction in being actively involved in their school career.

Teachers play a vital role in the development of the active learner. Below is a list of fifteen suggestions for teachers to use in helping students become active rather than passive learners.

1. Allow your students to think.

   Teachers want their students to think, but in their classrooms are students given enough opportunities to think? If only factual questions are asked (i.e.: What is the meaning of the word *loquacious*? What is the capital of Pennsylvania? Name three bones in the leg.), the teacher is depriving the students of vital opportunities to think. Could the heavy emphasis on factual questions be the reason why students get frustrated in school, begin to fail, feel inadequate and helpless, and eventually give up? Rather than take chances, create a classroom where opportunities for thinking abound. Listen to your students, encourage them to ask questions ("I expect you to ask questions"), be enthusiastic when they do ask questions, allow for divergent thinking, provide opportunities for discussion, and build their confidence. The way the learners

perceive themselves determines if they will be successful or not. If students see themselves as not being able to think or reason, they will begin to feel inadequate and become passive.

Entire texts are devoted to cognitive skills. Below are some questions that you can develop in your classroom to create the proper environment for developing thinking skills.

A. Let your students reason.
   ■ Emphasis: cause and effect relationships and giving reasons for outcomes or actions
   Why do you think...?

   How does _____ relate to

   _____ ?

   What are some reasons for _____ ?

   Why did _____ happen?

   How does _____ compare with

   _____ ?

   What do you see as the advantages and disadvantages of _____ ?

B. Let your students speculate, predict, and hypothesize.
   ■ Emphasis: developing plans to solve problems and presenting original ideas
   What will happen if _____ ?

   How do you think our country would function differently if we had no Congress?

   If you were President, how do you think you

   might solve _____ ?

   What kind of plan could we come up with

   to _____ ?

C. Let your students express their opinions, justify their choices, and judge the quality of something.
   ■ Emphasis: public confirmation of beliefs, making decisions, and discussions on how beliefs were arrived at
   Do you agree _____ ?

   What is your reaction _____ ?

What solution to _____ do you think would be the most efficient?

Who do you think is the greatest musician who ever lived?

2. Give all students time to think and formulate their answers. This "wait time" is so important, especially for students who have a harder time learning. Be patient with them. Let them know that you expect them to participate and that you will give them some time to gather their thoughts before you expect them to respond. Sometimes, teachers even expect the slower learner to respond **more** quickly. These teachers tend to be more tolerant with their "better" students, giving them more time and helping them along with their responses. Explain the wait time process to your students. Tell them that you are going to give them more time to think so they can come up with more complete and better answers. Tell them you want them to become **trained** reactive thinkers (see page 32). Then be sure that you reinforce longer, thoughtful answers and be sure **not** to reinforce short, incomplete answers.

3. Conduct daily and weekly reviews. This technique really gets the students involved in the learning process.

4. Call on every student. Don't just call on those students who have their hands raised. (Have a deck of index cards with students' names. Use these cards to call on students. After a student is called upon, put the card back into the deck so students know they may be called upon again during the class period. Another suggestion for making sure that all students respond is to mark off checks on a seating chart.) By calling on all of your students, you are saying to them, "All of you will be actively involved in my class *every day.*"

5. Tell your students what the objective of the day's lesson is. Call on students to restate the objective to be sure they understand.

6. Teach the material in small steps. Don't try to present too much material in one day. Allow students to experience success at each step.

7. Give students plenty of short practice sessions after each new concept is presented to be sure that they have grasped the material.

8. Show your students how new learning fits into what they have already learned. For instance, if students are learning about the American Revolution in history class, remind them of what they already know if you are going to study *Johnny Tremain* in English class.

9. Let your students know that you correct their work and that you use this information to check for understanding so you can either move on or reteach the material.

10. State your directions and assignments clearly. Have students repeat them to check their understanding. Encourage students to ask for clarification.

11. Encourage your students to keep an assignment book (What has to be done? What has to be handed in? When is it due?) and to follow a schedule (stressed in Chapter II).

12. Prepare "study guides" for your students related to their homework assignments. Study guides give students the structure they need to do homework. These guides can help your students to learn on their own. They are an essential tool for the student who has difficulty doing assignments. When you give an assignment, show your students *how* to complete it.
 Poor: Read Chapter 5 in your science book.
 Better: Read Chapter 5 carefully. List the three main points of the chapter. Define _____ , _____ , and _____ . Relate at least one point in the chapter to something you have already learned in Chapter 4. You are the master here. You know the material you teach. Make specific questions to accompany any reading assignment you give. Let the questions follow in the same order the material is presented. Be sure to include more than factual questions. Remember to create questions that will develop the reasoning, creative, and valuing skills of your students.

13. Help your students develop good listening skills. Make them aware of the important clues you give when you want them to know that something is important (page 46).

14. Encourage your students to develop a respect for their textbooks. Take time to go through the books with your students, pointing out significant parts (page 35).

15. Encourage your students to take notes (Chapter V deals in depth with notetaking). Taking notes helps the learner to be active. The students are forcing their ears, their hands, their eyes, and their minds to work together.

Remember—you are a very important person in developing active learners. Your students need your expertise, your time, and your patience.

Becoming an Active Learner

STUDENT INTRODUCTION

No one can make you an active learner. You have to accomplish this task yourself. Set a goal for yourself. Put your sights on becoming an active learner.

This section contains many activities that will help you reach your goal, but before you begin, you must realize that if you are going to be successful, you must be **interested** in what you are doing. Unless you allow it to happen, no one—no matter what he or she can do—can be interested for you. You have the power.

As you continue your education, you are going to study many subjects: some you will like immediately; others, you may find you have no interest for. Just because a subject proves to be difficult and requires a lot of work is no reason to be disinterested. Working hard at a subject which does not immediately appeal to you and discovering success can give you a wonderful reward: **Confidence.** This confidence will make you feel capable of handling work that is difficult and unexciting. In your lifetime there will be tasks that will be hard and unappealing, but if you learn the lesson now that not everything in life is easy, fun, and exciting, you are on your way to becoming a happy, well-adjusted student and person.

Accept these tasks which may seem unappealing and find something in them that **does** interest you—even if it is just the belief in your own ability to accomplish these tasks. Instead of thinking, ''This science project is going to be murder! There's no way I can get it done!'', substitute these thoughts, ''This science project may be murder, but if I plan a course of action and put some time and effort into it, I know I can get it done! And I'll bet I'll learn some things I never knew before!''

Get rid of the following statement from your vocabulary: ''It's boring!'' and replace it with ''This could be a real challenge!'' With this positive attitude you are now ready to begin the **Active Learner** workouts which will provide you with tips on thinking, textbooks, homework, and attitude. Accept the challenge for school and life!

WARM UP

Active learners think clearly. To become an active learner it is important to examine the thinking process. Now, let us examine two types of thinkers.

There are two basic types of thinkers, and these types affect the kind of person you are, both in and out of the classroom. **Reactive** thinkers are people who do not practice what they are going to say or do before they do it. They respond quickly to actions, and sometimes the responses are wrong. **Reflective** thinkers, on the other hand, do practice what they are going to say or do before they respond. They are slower to respond because they take the time to think about the next step.

Are you a reactive thinker or a reflective thinker? To understand the type of thinker you are, answer the following Work Out questions. Circle the correct answer.

WORK OUT

1. Do you blurt out things you sometimes wish you had never said?

   yes   no

2. Do you think carefully about questions before you respond?

   yes   no

3. Do you tend to get angry quickly and do things you regret later?

   yes   no

4. Do you think about a situation before you react?

   yes   no

5. Do you tend to "jump into things"?

   yes   no

6. Do you make decisions quickly only to change your mind later?

   yes   no

7. Do you like to think things over for a little while?

   yes   no

8. When you write, do you do any kind of preplanning? That is, make a list, outline, etc.

   yes   no

9. When you begin an assignment or a test, do you start right away?

   yes   no

10. Do you read assignments or tests over carefully before you begin?

    yes   no

11. As you write, do you often make word changes, possibly even changing entire paragraphs around?

    yes   no

12. Do you pause a lot while you are working to decide where to go next?

    yes   no

13. Do you reread your entire test over to yourself at least once when you are finished?

    yes   no

14. Are you usually satisfied with your assignments once you are finished?

    yes   no

15. Do you like to get the "chore" of writing, homework, or tests over with as soon as possible?

    yes   no

16. Do you raise your hand right away in class even if you are not sure of the answer?

    yes   no

BECOMING AN ACTIVE LEARNER

17. Do you make "easy" mistakes on tests because you tend to rush?

    yes   no

18. When you are learning something new, do you practice drills over and over until the new subject (sport or job) seems like you always knew it?

    yes   no

19. Do you take the time to practice a new exercise in your head, always thinking about different possibilities and how you would handle them?

    yes   no

20. Do you believe that "practice makes permanent"?

    yes   no

Think about your answers. "Yes" answers to question numbers 1, 3, 5, 6, 9, 15, 16, and 17 indicate that you are a reactive thinker. Reactive thinkers need to learn how to slow down so they can give their minds the time to process the information. There is nothing wrong with needing a little more time to think; there is something wrong if you don't give your mind the amount of time it needs.

If you answered "yes" to questions 2, 4, 7, 8, 10, 11, 12, 13, 18, 19, and 20, you are probably a reflective thinker. Reflective thinkers are generally more mature thinkers. They know the importance of taking time to process information, and their schoolwork and other activities show the extra time that they put into doing them.

Question number 14 can refer to both reactive and reflective thinkers. Why?

Active learners know the situations where they need to be reactive thinkers and the situations where reflective thinking is essential. In some activities, you do have to train yourself to become a good reactive thinker. For instance, if you were driving a car or participating in a sport, other people may react rather unfavorably if you required too much time before you reacted—in fact, it might even be dangerous. If you are in a math class, and your teacher asks you the answer to 5×5, she might react quite unfavorably if you took thirty-five seconds to respond. Consequently, this is where practice, drill, and mental rehearsal come in. When you practice and practice until you have almost "overlearned" your subject, you have trained yourself to react intelligently. In these situations, you don't need all of the reflecting time because you have practiced beforehand. You can react quickly and effectively if you have prepared. In situations where you need to reflect, to consider, to sort out information, you must learn to give yourself time. As you become more of an active learner, you will clearly see the situations where it is necessary to be reactive and the situations where reflection is necessary.

COOL DOWN

Think about it. How does the type of thinker you are affect you in school? How does it affect you in other activities? What can you do to help you either think more reflectively or become a trained reactive thinker? What other situations call for reactive thinking? What situations can you think of that would require reflective thinking? Be prepared to discuss your responses with your classmates.

WARM UP

Active learners also respect their textbooks and become very familiar with what they contain. Learn to respect your textbook. Realize that it has many important pieces of information in it. The book that you use in class is very important. It helps you to train for success in your studies. Use the frame in the Work Out to help you to get to know your textbook: the better you know your book, the better you will understand what you read.

WORK OUT

Directions: First, carefully read the following textbook frame on page 35. Then make a list of the information you can use to fill in the blanks. Next, make a copy of the textbook frame and fill in the blanks with your best information. Give as much information as possible. Try not to give one-word answers. You may even need to add several words or sentences. When you are finished, you should have a well-developed six-paragraph report on one of your textbooks.

Checklist:

Did you use as many specific details as possible about your book?

Did you read your response out loud either to yourself or someone else to be sure it makes sense?

Be prepared to read your response to the class.

COOL DOWN

If your textbook has an index at the end, pick five items that are listed. Copy the items and their page numbers down. Check the actual pages of your book to see if those items appear where they should. If your textbook does not have an index at the end, can you explain why the author(s) felt it wasn't necessary?

My _____ Book Is a Valuable Tool

_____ is the name of my _____ book. It was

written by _____ in the year _____ .

On page _____ I found some information about the author. I think

_____ wrote this book because _____ .

This _____ book is _____ pages long. It is divided

into _____ chapters and/or units. There are/are not many pictures and

illustrations in each chapter. The pictures are very _____ to look at

because _____ .

Some useful guides to help me understand what I read also appear in my book.

Throughout each chapter, there are (exercises, headings, definitions, questions, short

summaries, etc.). These are helpful because _____ .

At the end of each chapter, I notice _____ . Also, at the end of the

book, I can find (a glossary, index, etc.). I can use this whenever _____ .

I hope this book will help me understand _____ . I know that if I

_____ , _____ , _____ , I will do

well in _____ .

A Common Sense Approach to Homework

WARM UP

Active learners realize that there are certain responsibilities that must be accepted and one of them is doing homework. Homework doesn't have to be a bad word if you come to realize that homework helps to make learning more enjoyable and that it gives you the opportunity to continue to develop your thinking skills outside of the classroom.

In Chapter II you examined how to control your physical and mental environment to make learning more enjoyable. You have probably begun to make and follow schedules, have tried to shut out distractions, and have made an attempt to organize all of your study equipment. Good work. In this exercise, more tips will be presented to help you begin to accept the responsibility of homework with a positive attitude, and maybe even a smile.

WORK OUT

Part 1. Carefully read the suggested homework tips in the box below.

- Have a set time for doing homework.
- Tackle the hardest subject first.
- Write down the assignment when it is given and list the date it is due.
- Keep your homework organized in a notebook or folder.
- Use your best handwriting. Your handwriting should be neat and easy to read. People want to be able to read *what* you have written.
- Use a colored pen, pencil, or highlighter to underline key words or ideas in your notes or the books you personally own.

Part 2. Make _____ copies of the homework reminder form below. Follow it for _____ days.

My Homework Reminder Form

Date _____

Subject _____

Due on _____

I must read or study the following:

_____

I must write or do the following:

_____

I must bring home the following:

_____

Other important information about the assignment:

_____

_____

COOL DOWN

Interview three people (parents, friends, teachers, relatives, administrators, etc.) and ask them to share at least one "tip" they have for doing homework. Write these tips down on a 3 × 5 card. Be prepared to share some of these tips with the class.

"Quotable Quotes"

WARM UP

An active learner possesses many important qualities—many that you already possess and other qualities that you can make your own if you are just willing to try. This Work Out examines, in a unique way, some of the characteristics of an active learner.

WORK OUT

A fictional author, Taylor B. Temple, has just completed over fifty interviews for his new book entitled *Lifestyles of the Active Learner*. Read the statements below made by some of the active learners he spoke to. These are statements you may have made yourself or would like to make. These are definitely statements to be proud of. Say them and mean them. If you mentally rehearse them enough, you will start to improve your attitude toward learning and life.

"I'm not afraid to ask questions."
Ella Martinez

"I love to learn new things."
Cara Beachman

"I take responsibility for my actions."
Justin Andrews

"I feel good when I do well in school."
Kevin Seftwicki

"I like getting things finished."
Yoko Kim

"I am dependable."
John Michael Fitzpatrick

"I remember to get things done on my own."
Philip Berneau

"I feel proud when I know that others can count on me."
Anne Charney

"I am not afraid of hard work."
Jeff Eisner

"I can take a task, discover a way to handle it, and get it done on time."
Cicely Jefferson

"I'm not afraid to take time to think before I answer a question."
Marena Ragnacci

"I'm not afraid to express my beliefs and tell how I arrived at them."
Katie Prezkop

"I keep my school work organized."
T.J. Marler

"I'm persistent; I won't give up."
Ross Morosky

COOL DOWN

Select your three favorite quotes from the list above and explain why you feel that they are important statements for a student who cares about being an active learner. Be prepared to discuss your explanations with the class.

Help a Friend

WARM UP

Successful students are active students. They pay attention, they listen carefully, they think, they ask questions, they treat their textbooks as valuable sources of information, they do their homework, and they want to learn. In previous exercises you have examined how to become an active learner. Can you use this information to help someone who is having difficulty in school? Yes, you can—have confidence. Try the Work Out below.

WORK OUT

Carefully read the diary entry below of Lazy Lars (*lazy:* adj. not willing to work or be active). He can be classified as a lazy learner, but he doesn't know why. Make a list of all the reasons why he is not an active learner. Then, write an inspirational letter to Lars telling him how he can become a more active learner. He needs your encouragement. (Hint: Don't forget to refer back to the other exercises to get suggestions.)

COOL DOWN

Exchange your letter with a classmate. Compare the suggestions you made in your letter with those of your classmate. Were they alike? What other information could you have included that you didn't? What did you like best about your classmate's letter? Be prepared for a class discussion on the advice you gave.

Dear Diary,

My parents and teachers expect too much from me! My grades are not very good in school, and everyone keeps telling me to do better. Imagine being told to clean up my desk and sort through all my schoolwork! What does neatness have to do with grades?

People just can't understand that it is impossible for me to do better. It's hopeless! Today, for instance, I tried very hard to pay attention during science class, but it was hard to stay awake. I kept dreaming about the movie I saw on television last night. Then, when I started to yawn, my teacher thought I was raising my hand. When she called on me, I didn't even know the question. Boy, I hate feeling stupid. That's why I never raise my hand in class.

Later, the kids who wanted to work on projects divided into groups. Nobody even asked me, but I don't care. Those projects sound like an awful lot of hard work. But I did overhear them talking about me. I wonder why they call me Lazy Lars?

The Magic of ''If''

WARM UP

Developing your thinking skills, getting to know your textbook, and organizing and completing assignments will all help you to become an active learner. You will reap rewards by being an active learner: Learning will be challenging and exciting, schoolwork will become easier, grades will improve, and you will begin to feel better about yourself. You will be in control. You will be actively involved in your school career. You won't fail; you will succeed. Accept the challenge to be an active learner.

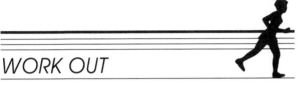

WORK OUT

Now try to imagine the consequences if the following situations occur. Read all the sentence starters below. Then, complete each sentence starter in the next column with as many consequences as you can.

Example: If I'm not afraid to be wrong,...

I will answer more questions in class.

I will ask about things that confuse me.

I will often give right answers.

I will not get that sick, queasy feeling inside before I answer a question.

I will learn more.

1. If my teacher gives me a little more time to respond to questions,...

   _____

2. If I listen carefully to directions,...

   _____

3. If I get to know the parts of my textbook,...

   _____

4. If I take the time to think before I speak,...

   _____

5. If I ask questions,...

   _____

6. If I become an active learner,...

   _____

COOL DOWN

Make a list of the three suggestions from the active learner section that you think will be most helpful to you in becoming a better student. Write them on a 3 × 5 card and mentally rehearse them as often as you can. They will soon become an important part of your strategy to become a more active learner.

A Training Program for Effective Notetaking

TEACHER INTRODUCTION

SUGGESTIONS FOR USING THIS CHAPTER

Consider this: students spend anywhere from 60 percent to 90 percent of classroom time listening—listening to readings, teacher lectures, etc. Yet, students are rarely taught how to develop their listening skills and how to take notes on what they hear.

Teachers can address this problem and help their students learn how to listen more effectively and how to sort the information that they hear into notes. In this chapter the focus for the students will be on four major areas:

1. Listening skills
2. Taking and organizing notes from a lecture
3. Taking and organizing notes from a book
4. Reviewing notes for learning

As mentioned in Chapter IV, students' minds need to be kept actively engaged; they need to be kept busy while they are in the process of listening. Listening—just like speaking, reading, and writing—is a language-based competency. The skill must be mastered so that effective communication can be achieved. Listening is a thinking skill and it can be taught.

By teaching our students how to listen, we are fostering their thinking. We are teaching them to search—with their minds—for main ideas and important details, to disregard the irrelevant, to note an organizational strategy and follow it, and even to make predictions about what the speaker will say or do next. Consequently, although listening has been termed a "receptive" act, listening does require the mind to be quite actively engaged in order for information to be processed effectively.

Strategy. However, just like the development of any skill, teachers must commit themselves to a structured and sequential strategy in order to train their students in effective listening and notetaking skills. The actual classroom routine is very important, as noted in Chapter II. All content teachers should work together in devising a systematic, school-wide plan for listening and notetaking. At the beginning of the year, teachers and students can work at 5-10 minute daily practice sessions in notetaking. That is,

after the short practice session, students can exchange notebooks and make comparisons. Then, teachers can illustrate, either on the board or with a handout, what important ideas and details should be in the notes. After the initial weeks, notebook checks could be made periodically throughout the content chapters.

Classroom Routine. The classroom routine should be consistent, as well. Managing an effective classroom is usually a three-step process: the Warm Up, the Work Out, and the Cool Down, also known as the "Wrap Up." In the Warm Up, teachers give students the "big picture," the overall focus of the class. Students are prepared for the lesson because they know what to expect, what they will learn, and why it is important. At this time, content teachers also do experiential background checks and try to fill in the gaps that might exist. For instance, a background check in a science class might reveal that certain key vocabulary words or concepts may need to be explained so that some students are not at a disadvantage during the lecture.

During the Work Out, teachers can keep the various types of learners (see Chapter I) in mind and use strategies to accommodate them during the lecture. For example, the use of charts, an outline on the board, or other visual aids would help the visual learner. Again, students need to be kept actively engaged for optimal learning, and they should be doing something to assure this engagement takes place. Discuss with students the importance of notetaking. Show them how to take good notes and work with them. Some form of notetaking is imperative, and there are a number of effective notetaking strategies. For students who are just learning the skill, the partially completed student outline is ideal. The outline can be constructed in a variety of ways as long as it follows the lecture format. Students fill in the gaps in the outline with their own words throughout the lecture, and at the end teachers can check the results.

Although outlining is a very valuable skill, students have to be taught not to misuse it, especially if they tend to copy the lecturer's exact words. Rewording the speaker's words during outlining or notetaking is imperative because it not only requires the students to think about relationships, but it also requires them to think about the actual meaning. If they can put the material in their own words, they have understood what was said. Give students practice time and check their work. Stop after a few minutes of lecturing or reading and have them write a short summary (two or three sentences). Let students share their summaries and compare with other students or a model summary. Put several effective summaries on an overhead or a handout and go over them.

Students also must learn to recognize signal words and what they indicate. Most grammar books contain lists of such signal or transition words. Expose your students to these lists to help them in the reading, writing, and listening processes. Students have to realize that these words are very important during these processes because these words help them to identify the organizational plan of the writer or speaker. Also, how many times have students failed to recognize a teacher's individual signals? For instance, a teacher might say "Now, class, this is important..." or "Pay attention. You might see this again...."

When teachers use A.V. materials in their respective content areas, prepared preview sheets help the students understand the significance of the presentation. The preview sheets might be in the form of a study guide with questions related to the viewing that are to be answered, or the sheet could be a skeleton outline that requires the students to fill in the details and facts. Whatever strategies teachers incorporate, students need to be prepared beforehand to enhance their listening for optimal learning.

The Cool Down period of each class is the "Wrap Up." Here, teachers summarize the major points that were covered, remind students of what they learned and why, and/or even conduct a quick review.

Consistency, structure, sequence of skills and classroom routine are important aspects of effective education. When students are instructed in a consistent **training program** for effective notetaking and listening skills that they can apply in every context, the students will be more prepared to digest the new information that is presented each day and less likely to feel overwhelmed. It is possible to train students to be effective listeners and notetakers; the activities in this chapter make this task easier.

A Training Program for Effective Notetaking

STUDENT INTRODUCTION

Learning how to listen and how to sort the information that you hear are important activities whether you are in school or not.

If you know how to listen and if you know what to do with the information that you hear, you are on the road to success. It is never too late to improve! In this section of the *Study Skills Workout*, you will learn the skills to help you become an effective listener and notetaker. You will focus on four major areas:

1. Listening skills

2. Taking and organizing notes from a lecture

3. Taking and organizing notes from a book

4. Reviewing your notes for learning

Continue with the training program. Perk up your ears, sharpen your pencils, and believe that you can became a skilled listener. Chapter V of this **WORKOUT** will enable you to start on the road to school success and learn skills that will help you on your lifelong journey to acquiring new information.

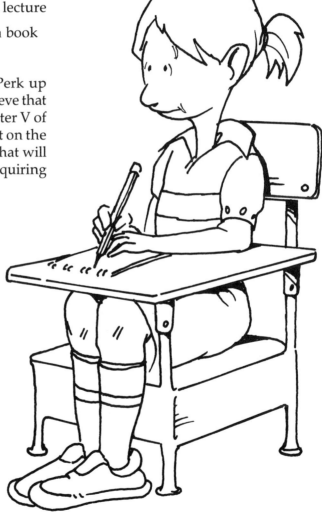

WARM UP

Listening is a skill that is important not only in school but also in many other areas of your life. Think about it—following directions is a listening skill. You need to know how to follow directions in your schoolwork, when you are driving a car, or when you are attempting any task that is unfamiliar to you. Can you think of any recent times that you needed to listen better in order to avoid making an important mistake?

Is hearing the same as listening? You may be able to hear the voices of your teachers, but do you really listen to what they have to say? Are you paying attention or is your mind drifting off to a favorite daydream?

Building strong muscles is hard work. Building strong listening skills is hard work, too, but you can do it! You must discipline yourself to **concentrate** on what your teachers have to say. When you concentrate, you are "taking in" the information that is being presented and directing it to a special place in your mind where you will make sense out of it and store it until you need to use it again.

WORK OUT

For this Work Out session, answer the questions on page 45. Circle the number 3 (Always), 2 (Sometimes), or 1 (Never) for each question related to how well you listen. Then, when you are finished, total your scores to see how well you have trained yourself to listen. Remember: This questionnaire is made to help you think about your listening skills.

Add your scores. Rate yourself according to the chart below.

27–30 points	Superior
24–26 points	Above Average
20–23 points	Average
16–19 points	Below Average
15 or below	Needs Improvement

Make a list. Brainstorm on how you can improve your listening skills and compare your list with a classmate.

COOL DOWN

A. Be prepared to read an informative paragraph out loud to your classmates. Then make up five questions about the paragraph and ask your classmates to answer them. After they have written down their answers, read the paragraph again. Check the answers. How well did your classmates listen?

B. Make a maze out of the classroom desks. (Be sure to ask your teacher first.) Blindfold one student and have another student give the student oral directions to get through the maze.

	ALWAYS	SOMETIMES	NEVER
1. Do you get ready to listen as soon as the signal to start class has been given?	3	2	1
2. Do you establish eye contact and watch your teachers closely when they are speaking?	3	2	1
3. Do you listen to your teacher's directions for a homework assignment and write them down?	3	2	1
4. If you don't understand something your teacher says, do you ask for an explanation?	3	2	1
5. Do you stop to realize that your teachers work hard to present material to you?	3	2	1
6. When you catch yourself daydreaming, do you fight the temptation and begin to pay attention again?	3	2	1
7. Do you take notes in class to help you listen better?	3	2	1
8. Do you put the information into your own words?	3	2	1
9. Do you listen to your classmates when they ask your teacher questions or when they respond to a question?	3	2	1
10. Do you believe that you can always learn something new?	3	2	1

A TRAINING PROGRAM FOR EFFECTIVE NOTETAKING

WARM UP

When you are taking notes, you may want to write down what the teacher says, but you may find that you get very nervous trying to copy **everything** down. The result—you miss many important things that have been said, and your notebook has a lot of unimportant information. Most teachers help to solve your problem by using important words or phrases that **signal** you to copy down certain pieces of information. Keep in mind that these signal words are very similar (if not the same) as the signal words you use in reading and writing. As you become familiar with your teachers, you will start to realize the special words and ways they introduce important information.

WORK OUT

Think about it. How many times has a teacher said, ''Now class—you **might** see this again...'' or, ''For your test **tomorrow**...''? What do you think these signals mean? These are examples of signal words, and very often students do not take note of them.

In this Work Out, read the phrases below. Imagine that the signals and other words have come out of lectures by your teachers. Place a check by the clues you hear your teachers use. You might want to add other clues that your teachers use, as well.

☐ 1. You might see this on a test...

☐ 2. The first reason is...

☐ 3. Don't forget this...

☐ 4. You must remember...

☐ 5. Another example is...

☐ 6. Let's review this again...

☐ 7. Listen to the following and see if you can tell me...

☐ 8. Therefore...

☐ 9. Last week I mentioned that...

☐ 10. In summary...

☐ 11. The results were...

☐ 12. In conclusion...

☐ 13. An important point is...

☐ 14. It is important that you know this...

☐ 15. You'll need to know this later...

☐ 16. The causes of the war were...

☐ 17. Pay close attention to...

☐ 18. The four reasons are...

☐ 19. The three main points are...

☐ 20. For tomorrow...

COOL DOWN

A. What are some signals you use when speaking with your friends to signal that some important information will follow? Write them down. Share them with a classmate.

B. Watch (and listen to) the evening news. What signals does the announcer use to give the important details and facts?

Note This! (Part 1)

WARM UP

1. Notetaking is and will be a very important part of your school career.

2. Taking notes helps you to sort out the new information that is presented to you so you can remember it and use it again.

3. Taking good notes can save you many hours of study time.

4. If you can learn how to take neat notes and organize them effectively, you can improve your grades and have more time for yourself.

WORK OUT

See if you can help the five students on page 48 who are having problems with their notes. Read their problems. Then, select a solution number from the solution file. Place the solution number next to the problem.

COOL DOWN

Write each solution on a separate 3 × 5 index card. Result: You will have four helpful hints for good notetaking right at your fingertips. Review the tips often and check your "old" notes to see what improvements you can make.

Problem A — *Solution* ___
Maura Miser crowds all of her notes together. She does not leave any space on her paper. Every nook and cranny is covered with notes.

Problem B — *Solution* ___
Steven Short uses so many different abbreviations on his notes that when he goes to review them he is confused.

Problem C — *Solution* ___
Haroldo Halfway takes pretty good notes, but when test time comes around, he can't locate some of his notes because he accidentally filed one page of his social studies notes in his science folder! He forgets to study some of his notes because he thinks he was already tested on them.

Problem D — *Solution* ___
Nancy Noteitall copies down every single word her teacher says. Since she can't keep up, she winds up having papers filled with a lot of words but not much meaning. She claims that she never knows what is important.

Problem E — *Solution* ___
Conrad Confident thinks he takes pretty good notes. But his test grades are not what he would like them to be. In fact, he doesn't even know where some of the test questions have come from because he has never even heard of them before.

Solution #1
Always put the subject title on each page. Always put the date on each page. Always number the pages in the upper right-hand corner.

Solution #2
Compare your notes with a classmate's who consistently does better on the tests. What is missing in your notes? Or, ask your teacher to check over your notes to look for missing information.

Solution #3
Listen attentively so you can discover important information. Most teachers give clues (see page 46). Listen for them: ''Remember this...'' ''First...second...'' ''This is important...'' ''The causes are...'' ''The results are...'' ''Don't forget...'' etc.

Solution #4
Use abbreviations and symbols that you can understand and clearly recognize. If you make up your own abbreviations or symbols, make sure you have a key that explains them. (Example: * means **important**.)

Solution #5
Leave plenty of space between each line of notes so that your notes are easy to read. Also, you'll have room if you have to go back and add more information. Don't write notes in the margin; leave this space if you have to make additional notations later.

Answers: A-5, B-4, C-1, D-3, E-2

WARM UP

To do well in just about anything, you must learn to listen, follow directions, and "store" information until you are ready to use it. To be a good student, you must learn to "store" your information in the form of notes. In fact, good notetakers are not born—they are trained. You can train to become a good notetaker. Get ready for Part 2 of this Work Out.

WORK OUT

See if you can help the students below who are having problems with their notes. Read their problems on page 50. Then, select a solution number from the solution file. Place the solution number next to the problem.

COOL DOWN

Write each solution on a separate 3 × 5 card. Result: You will have five more helpful hints for good notetaking right at your fingertips. Check your "old" notes and habits and see what improvements can be made. Review the tips often.

Problem A — *Solution* ___
Cara Careless takes notes on all surfaces. She uses bits of scrap paper. She writes notes on her book covers and even her hands!

Problem B — *Solution* ___
Sonya Scatter keeps some of her English notes with some of her science notes, and some of her science notes with some of her math notes, and some of her math notes....

Problem C— *Solution* ___
Peter Plagiarism copies notes from a book almost word for word and forgets to give credit to the book or person he copied them from. Then, when he does a report, he copies his notes word for word. The report is not really his own, but it is someone else's.

Problem D — *Solution* ___
Ursula Underline underlines almost everything she reads. When she goes back to take notes, she can't tell what is important and what isn't.

Problem E — *Solution* ___
Conrad Complain thinks that his notes are only for studying—and he never studies them until the night before a test. Then he complains because he has too much to learn in one night, and he quickly forgets the material soon after the test. Boy, is he in trouble when a big review test comes up!

Solution #1
Keep each subject area's notes in one place. Your notes are invaluable. A folder or binder is a good safe place to store your notes. Make sure the subject is labeled clearly.

Solution #2
Read over your notes as soon as possible after class. Fill in any additional information if possible. Keep in mind that spending a few minutes reading your notes each day will mean all the more you will remember. When test time arrives, you will already know most of the information. You will also want to spend longer review periods starting a few days before the test. After the test is returned, go over the areas that you missed and double check your notes again. This will also save you time before a major review test.

Solution #3
Take your notes on clean, full-sized sheets of paper.

Solution #4
Underline only the important points to make them stand out. Don't mark up a page just for the sake of doing something—remember that notetaking is far more effective than underlining or highlighting. But if you do underline, look for important words, phrases, definitions, and dates. And, of course, only underline in books that belong to you.

Solution #5
Take notes in your own words. You will be able to remember something in your own words much easier than words that belong to someone else. However, if you do copy something from a book (even if it is in your own words), always write down the author, name of the book, and the page number. If you give proper credit to the person who actually wrote the material, then you will not be accused of **plagiarism** (using someone else's words or ideas without permission).

Answers: A-3, B-1, C-5, D-4, E-2

WARM UP

Taking good classroom notes is important, but taking good notes when you read a book is also very important. When your teachers say, "Read pages 56-59 for homework tomorrow," they don't just want you to flip through the pages. They want you to **remember** what you have read, and they want you to **understand** what you have read. There are ways to attack a reading assignment. Get ready to learn how.

WORK OUT

General U.R. Willing has just taken a course on how to read effectively, and he has agreed to share his secret file with you. Your assignment is to read his material over very carefully. He has divided his information into three categories: "before you read," "while you read," and "after you read."

SECRET FILE

Before you read...

1. look over the material. Check to see how many pages you have to read. Are there words defined at the bottom of the pages? Are there questions at the end of each section? If so, read them so you will have an idea of what you have to look for when you read.

2. pay attention to the signs that your textbook might give you. Pay close attention to categories like **main points, summaries, chapter checkups, important facts,** etc.

While you read...

1. pay attention to **boldface type** and *italics* because they signal important information.

2. study charts, tables, graphs, and pictures. Remember to read the captions under the pictures.

3. make a list of words that you don't understand. Look them up in your dictionary or glossary.

4. you may want to stop at the end of each paragraph and outline what you have read, or write a short summary in your own words. This way you will be sure to understand as you go along and you will remember much more.

5. you may get tired. If you do, take a short break. Rest your eyes and stretch your muscles. But try not to take a break before you have worked twenty minutes.

After you read...

1. carefully read the questions at the end of the chapter or section. If you can't answer them, go back and reread the section again.

2. go back and make a set of notes for yourself on the material you have just completed. Read these notes over and recite them out loud to a friend, a relative, or yourself!

COOL DOWN

Select one of your textbooks. Then, pick a chapter. What signs does your chapter give you to point out the important information (boldfaced words, questions, etc.)? Copy down the types of signs you find. Be prepared to share your findings with the class. If you are really ambitious this week, find the signs in every textbook you use.

WARM UP

Outlining is one effective way of taking good book notes. Because outlining makes you look for the main ideas and the details which support the main ideas, outlining really exercises your mind as you read. It forces you to organize the facts and details that you are reading. It also helps you to remember what you have read because you are putting the information in your own words.

WORK OUT

Keep in mind that there are many effective ways to outline. Some people like to use Roman numerals, some do not. Some people follow the structure of a formal outline, but other people use an informal outline. It is important to know what your teacher requires. Your teachers will show you how they will want you to outline in their classes. Pay close attention to their instructions.

If your teacher does not require you to use a formal outline, but you are not remembering what you read, then you have to look for a better way to take notes. Taking notes when you read from a textbook is an important skill to learn. This Work Out will show you how one student outlined the information from a social studies chapter.

1. Carefully read the selection listed below on state government.

2. Next, look over the sample outlined notes on page 54.

3. Pay close attention to the explanations that are given in the margins.

4. Then, go back to the selection and notice how the information in the outline mentions the important details in the paragraphs. Note, too, how the student put the information in her own words.

5. Are there any additional facts that you think should be included in this outline?

Lesson 1   State Government

Each of the 50 states has its own government. The home of a state government is the state capital. What city is your capital? Find the answer on pages 340-341.

State governments need laws to follow. Each state has its own set of laws. They are given in the state's **constitution**. The voters in the state approved their constitution. They agreed to go by the laws in it. From time to time they may decide to change or add to it. Any changes must be voted on. One reason we say that our government is a democracy is because voters have a chance to decide on the laws of their state.

The constitution tells how the state government is to work. There are three parts in the state's government. Each part has certain duties. Each has powers the other parts don't have. This is a way to keep any one part from becoming too strong or powerful.

The Governor

The governor's office is one part of state government. The governor is the leader of the state government. The governor makes sure the state's laws are carried out. This is an important part of the governor's job.

From Dr. Barbara M. Parramore and Dan D'Amelio, *Scott Foresman Social Studies* (Glenview, Illinois: Scott, Foresman and Company, 1979), pp. 261-264. Copyright © 1979 Scott, Foresman and Company.

The governor is elected by the voters of the state. New people to the state have to become residents before they can vote. State laws say when and how a person becomes a **resident.** Laws also say how a person becomes a voter.

Highway safety is a big duty of the governor. He or she has many workers helping the people follow the traffic and safety laws. These workers remind people to follow the laws. They report people who do not follow the laws. Sometimes they suggest changes in the law, such as lower highway speeds near a school. Then the governor asks the legislature to make a new law. It takes time to make changes in the law. However, changes can be made with hard work and time when there is a need.

The Legislature

The governor cannot make a law. The **legislature** can. In each county or parish or borough, the people vote on members of the legislature.

The people choose the leaders they want. Then they send the leaders to the state capital to make laws. Voters can make suggestions to their **legislators.** Legislators like to get letters and telephone calls from the people.

Suppose the governor tells the legislature a new highway law is needed. Suppose you and your family wrote a letter to your legislator. You say there should be a new highway law too. The new law would then have been suggested by the governor and by the voters. The legislators decide there must be a real need for the law. They vote to pass the law. After that, it must be followed by all people.

The legislature decides what a crime is. It also decides how people who break laws should be punished. Have you seen a highway sign like this: "No littering, **offenders** will be fined $50.00."? The legislature decided on two things. One was that a law was needed to stop littering. Another was how to punish people who do not obey this law. The sign tells about both laws.

State legislators are the rule-makers for a state. They decide what the laws are going to be.

Courts

Courts are a part of state government. Judges are important people in this part of the government. They study the constitution. They study laws passed by the legislature. They help see to it that laws are followed and lawbreakers are punished.

Suppose a large box of trash blew off a truck. The highway would be littered. The highway safety patrol officer would write a ticket telling who broke the law, the place, and the date. The lawbreaker would go to court.

In court, the judge would listen to the officer's report. The person charged would get time to tell what happened too. The judge would look at the law. All things would be considered or thought about. Then the judge would make a decision. The judge decides if a law was broken or not. Then the judge makes a decision on how the lawbreaker should be punished.

Main heading

Notice how the heading comes from the section heading in bold print

Sub headings

Include definitions of unfamiliar words

Includes examples that help explain the idea

Notice the empty spaces that are left

There is room to add additional information later on

Note how words in bold print are important enough to put in notes

I. **State Government—located in state capital**
  A. **Constitution** ←
     1. tells what state laws are
     2. tells how government is to work
     3. democracy—changes must be approved by voters
  B. **State government has three parts**
     1. Governor ←
     2. Legislature ← *Supporting details*
     3. Courts ←

II. **The Governor**
  A. **Leader of state government—makes sure laws are carried out**
  B. **Elected by voters who are residents**
     1. resident—person who lives in a certain place
     2. state laws
        a. tell how and when a new person can become a resident
        b. tell how a person can become a voter
  C. **Has many duties**
     1. Example—highway safety
     2. Governor can ask legislature to make new laws if they are needed.

III. **The Legislature**
  A. **Makes laws**
  B. **Voters choose members of legislature from each county, parish, or borough**
     1. Legislators—lawmakers such as senators and representatives
     2. voters can write and ask legislators to make new laws
  C. **Decides what a crime is**
     1. Example—littering
     2. Decides what punishment is needed for people who break laws

IV. **Courts**
  A. **Judges**
     1. study constitution and laws
     2. see that laws are obeyed and lawbreakers are punished
        a. Example—if a person is charged with littering

COOL DOWN

A. Read the paragraphs on page 55 taken from actual textbooks. Then, try to outline what you have read. (Remember to read the paragraph(s) first.) Compare your outline with a classmate's. Did you get all of the important details and information? Did you put your notes in your own words?

B. Try to outline a small section (one or two pages) from a textbook. Compare your outline with a classmate's. Did either of you miss any important information? Then, put your outline aside and take turns quizzing each other. Did you find it easier to remember what you had read after you took notes?

A TRAINING PROGRAM FOR EFFECTIVE NOTETAKING

Why Is Sleep Important?

Sleep also helps keep your body healthy. Scientists cannot explain exactly how sleep helps your body. If you do not get enough sleep, however, you will feel tired and restless. Sleep helps you feel alert and healthy.

When you sleep, many of your body processes slow down. Your pulse and breathing rate decrease. Your temperature lowers. Voluntary muscles relax.

Other body systems are active while you sleep. Your digestive system breaks down food. Your pituitary gland releases growth hormone while you sleep. Brain stem cells send impulses that cause you to dream. Scientists are studying the brain activity of the sleeping person in the picture. The scientists hope to learn how sleep helps the body function at its best.

From Michael R. Cohen. (et al.,) *Scott Foresman Science* (Glenview, Illinois: Scott, Foresman and Company, 1986), p. 184. Copyright © 1986 Scott, Foresman and Company.

Types of Natural Vegetation

Look at the map on page 66. It shows where certain types of natural vegetation grow in the Western Hemisphere. Factors such as climate, rainfall, and soil determine the types of vegetation that grow in a particular area. There are four general types of vegetation—forest, desert, grassland, and tundra.

Forests. Forests are found in many parts of the Western Hemisphere. There are several kinds of forests: softwood, hardwood, and rainforests.

Softwood forests are made up of evergreen trees, which keep their needlelike leaves all year. These forests are usually found in cold places. They cover much of Alaska and Canada. Some softwood forests grow in warmer places, such as the southeastern United States and northwestern South America.

Hardwood forests are made up mostly of trees that lose their leaves each winter. Such forests generally grow in warm, rainy places with long growing seasons.

Sometimes hardwoods and softwoods grow together in mixed stands. These mixed stands are common in the eastern half of the United States, western Canada, and in parts of central Mexico.

Rainforests grow near the Equator where rain is heavy most of the year. Some places in the Amazon region of South America receive over one hundred inches of rain a year. The Amazon is the world's largest forest region. The plants and trees there grow fast and thick. Most keep their broad, shiny leaves all year long. The Amazon rain-forests are so dense that hardly any light reaches the ground.

From Dr. Joan Schreiber. (et al.,) *Scott Foresman Social Studies: Western Hemisphere* (Glenview, Illinois: Scott, Foresman and Company, 1983), pp. 65, 67. Copyright © 1983 Scott, Foresman and Company.

WARM UP

How often have you heard the expression ''neatness counts''? Well, neatness certainly does count when you are doing something as important as notetaking. You must be able to read your own handwriting if you expect to study effectively. Make every effort to write legibly. If you do write sloppily because you're rushing to get information down, recopy your writing as soon as possible, while the information is fresh in your mind. Some students even make a point of recopying notes because they find it helps them to remember the material.

WORK OUT

Students #1 and #2 were in the same class listening to the same lecture, but you could never tell

by looking at their notes! Imagine that you are a teacher grading notebooks. What letter grade would you assign to each of these notes? Why?

COOL DOWN

Reviewing your notes is an important part of making the most out of all your hard work. Keep in mind that you will not be able to remember even 20 percent of what you have written down if you do not read it over as soon as possible after class. When you are reviewing your notes, write out those notes that are illegible and fix your abbreviations. Add additional information such as definitions, etc. If you are unsure about anything, check with the teacher or compare your notes with a friend's who does well in the class.

#1

Grade ___
Comment Corner:

#2

Grade ___
Comment Corner:

December 15th
The Call of the Wild
Chapter 6 : " For the 'Love of a Man' "
New Characters :
  Nig ⎫ John Thornton's dogs
  Skeet ⎭ They are kind to Buck.
"Black" Burton - a man who attacks Thornton,
    and who is nearly killed by Buck.
Hans and Pete - Thornton's partners
Jim O'Brien - Thornton's friend who lends him
    the money to make a bet.
Matthewson - a man who makes a bet with
    Thornton.

Main Ideas :
  ✓ Buck recovers under the protection of John
    Thornton
  ✓ John Thornton and Buck develop a strong
    and loving relationship in this chapter.

  Buck does three great things for John :
  1. Buck attacks Burton who pushed
     Thornton to the ground.
  2. He rescues Thornton from the rapids.
  3. He wins a bet for Thornton by pulling
     a 1,000 pound sled for 100 feet.

A TRAINING PROGRAM FOR EFFECTIVE NOTETAKING

Exercising Your Memory

TEACHER INTRODUCTION

In today's world the ability to know and use learned pieces of information is very important if we are going to function and succeed in an ever-changing society. Figures tell us that the amount of growth in information is doubling at faster and faster rates compared to the growth of information a decade or more ago. Quite simply, because of strides in science, industry, and technology there is more to know today than fifty or more years ago. People, both young and old, need to rely on knowing and utilizing vast amounts of information in order to assure their success. Therefore, helping students to improve their memories is a vital aspect of the teaching process.

Memory means more than rote recitation; it means to organize information in the brain so that it can be recalled and put to use at a later point. There are two basic forms of memory: short-term and long-term. A person who learns a fact, such as a telephone number, and then "forgets" it after the fact is used has stored that fact in the short-term memory bank. If the same telephone number is remembered for days, years, or even a lifetime, the number has been stored in the long-term memory.

It is easy to think of the brain as a road map: each piece of information is stored at a particular destination. The information is never erased, but sometimes our brain forgets how to retrieve the information or its location among all the brain cells. In other words, our brain never actually loses the information; it just can't be located.

Because of the vast amounts of information and the modern technology for putting that information at our fingertips, many educators wonder when and how memorization should be used. As a basic rule, memorization should be utilized for procedures that would take more time if the information were not readily available. Such procedures might include memorizing number facts, times tables, and spelling words and/or rules.

Memorization should not, however, be done at the expense of understanding the process. When students memorize, they generally learn facts and details—the **what, when,** and **where.** This sort of memorization never requires them to function at higher cognitive levels (see Chapter IV); they are not being required to understand the **how** and the **why**

of what they are learning. The ability to utilize information contained in the memory to make associations, generalizations, abstractions, and categorizations is effective use of memorization. This ability requires good memorizing techniques and study habits as well as the ability to concentrate.

The following list contains information related to memory which can help you to prepare your students for active participation in this chapter. It is important for students to have a better understanding of what memory is, how it works, and how to use it effectively.

1. Memory is closely related to performance; the more you remember, the better you will be able to do whether the goal is academic, athletic, musical, etc.

2. It is not uncommon to hear of students who memorize information for tests only to be unable to recall the supposedly learned information a day later. For optimal study (remembrance), students need to be able to concentrate and study in surroundings conducive for learning, to read effectively, to take effective notes (see Chapter V), and to express what they have learned in writing.

3. Some items are easier to remember than others. For instance, information we use often, information we understand, information we agree with, information we find interesting, and happy memories are easy to remember.

4. Other items are more difficult to remember. For example, names, dates, numbers, unpleasant memories, information that we find hard to believe or that we disagree with, and material we don't understand are harder to remember.

5. As mentioned in Chapter V, it is necessary to review notes and/or readings as soon as possible after class for maximum retention.

6. Overlearning material cannot be emphasized enough because it helps students to relate the information and make the necessary categorizations, abstractions, generalizations, and associations. Therefore, to overlearn the material students should review as often as possible. Teachers can help students review by conducting

class in a systematic way: review material from previous class, conduct short daily and weekly reviews, check for understanding, and show how the new material is related.

7. Usually, one type of memory is stronger than the other. (See Chapter I, ''Learning Styles.'') Although we rely on our senses to send information to our brains, most of us rely on either visual, auditory, or kinesthetic/tactile styles to remember information. Having a **strategy** can help us remember. For instance, when we understand how we learn best, we can use that strength to help us remember more effectively. The activities in this chapter will help you and your students to develop a strategy that will work. In order to determine which technique will be most successful for them, it is beneficial for students to understand what type of learning style they have (Chapter I).

8. After our senses send the information to our brain, our brain then has to decide how it is going to process the information and where the information is going to be stored (in long- or short-term memory). Actually, it is the processing—what we do with the information once we have it—that determines how long we will remember what we have learned. When information is not put into active use, it becomes lost quite easily. Students are more likely to retain what they have learned when they are required to process the information on higher cognitive levels (Chapter V).

9. Interest plays an important part in the ability to memorize (Chapter IV). What we are interested in is easy to remember; what doesn't interest us is easy to forget. When students (and teachers) work hard to make a subject or area meaningful and interesting, they will be more likely to remember the information.

10. An effective way to learn a new subject (task, skill, etc.) is to teach it to someone else. Collaborative learning has many strengths because it encourages concentration, consistency, and organization. Students are encouraged to perceive and use what they have learned in yet another form of processing. Pairing students for teaching and/or review can help them **overlearn** the material and exercise different modalities for learning (Chapter I).

11. In the middle grades it is extremely important to take class time to show your students how to study. If you want them to remember a list of inventors with their inventions, show them different ways they can study the list. Remind them of the various memorization techniques presented in this section. The exercises are constructed to make students aware of the power of their memory. Exercising one's memory during the entire school year in every subject area can lead to very positive results.

12. Teachers have a vital role in showing students that they are not alone in the learning process; there are ways to improve memory. All methods may not work for all students, but students should understand how their memory works and how it can be improved. The students should be required to try the methods included in this chapter.

Exercising Your Memory

STUDENT INTRODUCTION

You own something that is very powerful—your memory. The power of your memory helps you to survive in this world. Think about it. What if you couldn't remember where you lived? What if you couldn't remember that you had to be careful when crossing a busy street corner?

Your memory allows you to remember a favorite player's batting average, a friend's favorite color, a special birthday, or the telephone numbers of a dozen friends or more. It helps you to recall the faces of your relatives, the colors of a rainbow, and the smell of freshly popped popcorn.

But sometimes your memory is not as strong as you would like it to be. Is your dental appointment at 4:30 or 5:30? Do you have to do page 14 or 15 for homework? What did your mother ask you to do after school? What is the capital of California?

You can improve your memory, but first you need to have a **plan.** This chapter of the **WORK-OUT** will show you several plans that will help you remember what you have learned. Although there are many plans, you are the one who must discover which plan will work the best for you. This chapter will cover the following areas:

1. Why Remembering Is Important

2. How to Use Your Memory to Learn

When you are finished with this chapter, you will understand just how powerful a good memory can be. The ability to store information in your brain and locate it when you need it is very important.

Why Remember?

WARM UP

Wanting to remember plays a large role in your ability to remember. You have to look at new information and say, "I **want** to remember this."

Remember how to set goals from Chapter III? When you set a goal, you have to know what you want, why you want it, and how you are going to get it. Making your memory stronger is a lot like goal setting. You have to know what you want to remember, why you want to remember it, and the rewards you will get from remembering.

One of the first steps in improving your memory is understanding the reasons for remembering the information.

WORK OUT

Here is a list of possible reasons for remembering information. Rank them in the order of their importance to you (use 1 for most important, and so on). Be prepared to discuss why some reasons are more important than others.

____ to get better test grades

____ to make my parents happy

____ to do the best job that I can

____ to make me feel good about myself

____ to prevent possible failure

____ to give me the knowledge or training I need to reach a personal goal

____ to impress my teachers and friends

____ to be able to do well outside of school

____ to show that I am "growing up" and I can handle responsibility

____ to enjoy life more

COOL DOWN

After you finish ranking the reasons for remembering information, compare your lists with two of your friends' lists. Discuss the differences. State why you listed something first, second, or last. Ask your friends why they ranked the various reasons the way they did. What did you learn from your discussion?

How Do I Remember?

Your brain is an amazing source of power! It is the master control center of your body. Your senses feed it information, and then your brain decides what to do with all the new information. It stores information from your past, and it produces new thoughts and ideas out of new information it receives. Your brain not only controls **what** you think but it also controls **how** you feel—your moods and emotions.

Although your brain only weighs about three pounds, it is a very complicated control center. Your brain is a lot like a road map. Every piece of information is sent to a specific destination in your brain. When your brain wants to remember something, it has to travel along the paths until it can find that piece of information.

Your brain has two memories—**short-term** memory and **long-term** memory. When you store information in your short-term memory, you lose it very quickly. For instance, have you ever looked up a telephone number and then forgot it before you even dialed? That is because you stored it in your short-term memory.

When you store information in your long-term memory, you remember it for a very long time. For example, your telephone number should be stored in your long-term memory. Can you think of any other information that should be stored in long-term memory? Where do you usually store information that you studied?

One way to remember better is to become very interested in what you have to learn. It is easier to remember things that spark your interest. The more you know about a subject, the more it will interest you.

Another way to remember better is to use your preferred learning style. (Remember your learning style from Chapter I?) If you use a style that suits you, you will remember more.

WORK OUT

Here is a list of strategies that many people try when they want to remember information. Check the ones that you use. Don't worry about the stars yet. They will be explained to you in the Cool Down.

☐ I read the information very carefully.*

☐ I read harder material out loud to myself.**

☐ I write or recopy the information.***

☐ I look at new words until I can spell them.*

☐ I recite information until I can remember it.**

☐ I trace or copy words a few times until I can remember them.***

☐ If I want to learn more about something, I read about it.*

☐ If I want to learn more about something, I ask questions.**

☐ I read my notes over often.*

☐ I have someone else quiz me on what I have learned.**

☐ I make up a sample test, take it, and then correct it to see what I have learned.***

☐ I underline important information in my notes.***

☐ I study in a quiet place.**

☐ I study in a neat and well-organized area.*

☐ I study wherever I feel comfortable.***

COOL DOWN

Look at the items you checked in the Work Out.

* — usually indicates a visual learner—you remember best by ''seeing''

** — usually indicates an auditory learner—you remember best by ''hearing''

*** — usually indicates a kinesthetic/tactile learner— you remember best by ''doing''

Are you trying to remember or study in a way that suits your learning style? If you are not doing as well as you would like, then maybe you should take another look at the **way** you are trying to study. Review what you learned about learning style in Chapter I.

WARM UP

How can you remember word lists? What is an easy way to remember ideas that don't seem to have a connection?

Grouping is an easy way to code your memory. Memory codes allow you to store the new information you receive with the old facts you have already learned. Such codes are useful when you have to remember bits of information such as names, places, or lists.

WORK OUT

Here are some ways to code your memory. Read the following suggestions very carefully.

A. Group in alphabetical order (Daleville, Moscow, Pittsburg, Scranton, Wilkes-Barre).

B. Group like letters together (potatoes, peas, pork, peppers, popcorn, peanut butter, pears, *or* butter, bags, bones).

C. Pair items that go together (bacon and eggs, cheese and crackers, pretzels and soda).

D. Put items in categories (Vehicles: cars, boats, trucks, airplanes, bicycles *or* States: Ohio, Alaska, South Carolina, Mississippi, Texas).

E. Chunk long lists by putting three or four items together. (This is especially helpful with numbers: 314-876-5389.)

F. Make a word out of the beginning letters of words you have to remember (**HOMES**— this word helps you to remember the names of the five Great Lakes—Huron, Ontario, Michigan, Erie, Superior).

G. Make a sentence out of the beginning letters of words you have to remember (**A r**at **in the** **h**ouse **m**ight **e**at **t**he **i**ce **c**ream).

H. Make up a sentence or silly story to help you remember words or facts (Thirty days hath September, April, June, and November. All the rest have thirty-one, excepting February alone . . . .).

COOL DOWN

A. Pick a partner. Make a list of ten words. (You might want to use your spelling list words or other words you will need for a test.) Choose a memory code that you think will work for you from the Work Out. See how well each of you memorize the list. How long did it take each of you?

B. Here is an experiment to see how you concentrate best. While you are watching a TV show, have someone read you a list of seven colors. Then try to repeat the colors in the correct order. Next, have your partner make up a new list of seven colors. Go to a quiet place where there are no distractions. Listen to the colors again and then try to repeat the colors in the correct order. Which experiment was easier? Did it take longer to learn the colors in the noisy room or the quiet room? How did you make yourself concentrate?

Concentration is very important when you are trying to learn. When you study, you should try very hard to concentrate. Do not allow outside noise or other distractions to keep you from learning. Try not to take too many breaks. Schedule your breaks after every thirty minutes or so of study.

Picture Yourself (Part 1)

WARM UP

A poor memory is often a disorganized memory. Isn't it difficult to find something in a place that is messy and disorganized? Isn't it easier when items are neatly stored in special places? With the right organization, you can learn to store information so that you can find it when you need it.

Pictures help to organize our memory. Pictures help us to remember. For example, can you remember all the details of your fourth birthday? Maybe some of your memories are not very clear, but if you were able to see a photograph of your birthday celebration, you could probably remember many of the sights, smells, sounds, flavors, and feelings that you had on that day.

You usually remember more of what you see than what you hear or read. If you can change the things you hear or read into mental pictures, you might be able to recall them more easily.

A ''sound picture'' is one way to help you recall things more easily. You can make a ''sound picture'' by selecting a word that sounds like the word you have to remember and then imagining what the word looks like. For example, if you are studying some or all of the fifty states, you could use a ''sound picture'' to remember them. Here are a few examples:

INDIAN-Indiana

TAX-Texas   **PENCIL-Pennsylvania**

ARK-Arkansas

EXERCISING YOUR MEMORY

Remember it is important to be able to see your ''sound picture.'' Match the following ''sound picture'' words with the musical composers' last names.

1. sherbet

2. Moe's art

3. a back

4. straw

5. rock man

6. beet oven (an oven in which you would make beets!)

7. a handle

___ (Igor) Stravinsky

___ (Ludwig Von) Beethoven

___ (George Fredrick) Handel

___ (Wolfgang Amadeus) Mozart

___ (Franz) Schubert

___ (Sergei) Rachmaninoff

___ (Johann Sebastian) Bach

For some of you, your ability to change things you read or hear into ''sound picture'' names will be an important factor in developing your memory. See if you can think of a ''sound picture'' word for the last names of the following artists. Also, try to form a detailed mental picture of the ''sound picture'' name.

Examples: #1—Artist: William Hogarth
''sound picture'' word: a hoe
''I picture a hoe in a garden. Then, I picture a man named William using a hoe in his garden. Now, I can remember both the first and the last name!''

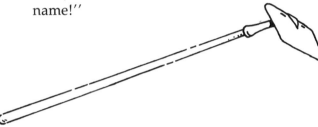

#2—Artist: Winslow Homer
''sound picture'' word: a home
''I see a home with *low* windows!''

Now, you are ready to try a few.

Salvador Dali
Norman Rockwell
Vincent Van Gogh
James Whistler
William Harnett

Picture Yourself (Part 2)

WARM UP

In the last exercise you saw how helpful it can be to organize material in your memory through pictures: In this exercise, you will learn more ways to help you create interesting pictures of items you have to learn.

The more senses you use to help you remember, the stronger your memory will become. In this exercise, you will practice using as many senses as possible to help you remember better.

WORK OUT

Read the following hints carefully:

A. Pretend that you are an actor or actress in the material you are learning—put yourself in the story.

> For example, if you are studying about George Washington crossing the Delaware, close your eyes and use your imagination. See George Washington crossing the Delaware. Feel the snow falling and the bitter cold temperatures. Hear the muffled oars and the water against the boats. How do his poorly dressed, cold men feel? What do they see, hear, taste, feel, and smell? (They surprised over 1000 Hessian soldiers at Trenton. It was December 25, 1776.)

B. If you are reading *The Adventures of Tom Sawyer* by Mark Twain, you can *be* Tom Sawyer or Becky Thatcher lost in the cave. What is it like in there? How will you get out? How do you feel?

C. If you have to learn the state flowers, imagine yourself in that state picking that particular flower. You are in Maryland picking black-eyed Susans.

D. You can also picture your favorite actor or actress as a major character in the material you are reading.

COOL DOWN

1. Picture yourself as a pilgrim in 1620 on the Mayflower. How do you feel? What do you see? What can you remember?

2. Picture yourself as a Union soldier during the Battle of Gettysburg. What can you hear? feel? see?

3. The next time you read a story, be sure to picture yourself as one of the major characters. Try to picture yourself at the scene whenever you can.

Association—One Way to a Better Memory

Do you remember silly things?

Another way to remember something is to link it with something that you already know. This is called association. It usually helps if the links or associations are "silly" or unusual. Try to imagine a silly or unusual picture of something you want to remember. The more silly or unusual your pictures are, the better they will work for you. Here are a few examples:

Example 1—A **baton** covered with red **rouge** and owned by a girl named **Louisa** could remind you that **Baton Rouge** is the capital of **Louisiana.**

Example 2—Imagining "a rat" in the word sep-*ara*te helps you to remember how to spell "separate."

Example 3—Kevin had to learn the following list of commonly used helping verbs for his English teacher. He made up a silly story filled with unusual pictures to help him remember the words in order. Kevin divided the list into sections and then made up a clue for each group of words.

Keep in mind that some associations may seem silly to you. In fact, this story may sound very silly to you, but it helped Kevin. He accomplished his task and did well. You might have a different way to learn lists. You have to find the way that works best for you.

A student is in school reciting the following:
- am
- is
- are
- was
- were

the *bell* rings to signal the end of the day
- be
- been

the student leaves school and stops to visit the *horses* at the stables
- has
- have
- had

because he spends so much time with the horses he doesn't study and gets D's on his report card
- do
- does
- did

he drowns his sorrows with m + m's
- may
- might
- must

the m + m's don't help — he needs more candy
- can
- could

he stops for a soda because he's thirsty from eating all the candy
- shall
- should

he walks home depressed
- will
- would

Your imagination is very important when you make associations. To make an association, simply change what you *hear* or *read* into something you can *see* in your imagination.

Here are some associations that are done for you. First, match the following "images" with the correct state capital. Then, try to name the state.

IMAGES

____ a fort made out of hot dogs guarded by a boy named Ken

____ a can of toes on top of a mountain peak

____ a knight named Mich holding a lance

____ a shy girl named Anne standing on the letter Y

____ a sack around a group of bare-toed men eating cauliflower

____ a hairy hamburger with a pencil stuck through it

CAPITAL

1. TOPEKA

2. SACRAMENTO

3. FRANKFORT

4. LANSING

5. CHEYENNE

6. HARRISBURG

(States: Kansas, Wyoming, Michigan, Pennsylvania, Kentucky, California)

COOL DOWN

Exercise your imagination. Make up clever associations for at least three of the following capitals and the country each represents.

Stockholm, Sweden
Tokyo, Japan
Belgrade, Yugoslavia
Madrid, Spain
Helsinki, Finland
Warsaw, Poland

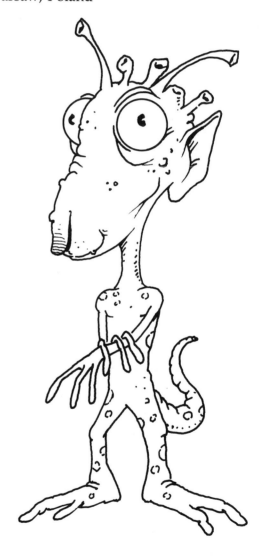

EXERCISING YOUR MEMORY

Schooling Your Memory

WARM UP

Meet Memma Rize, an alien from the planet Cerebellum. She has amazing memorizing powers. How does she do it? Read over her list of suggestions (some of the very same hints you learned from this chapter!). How many of them are you willing to try in order to improve your memory? Keep in mind that improving your memory means having a plan and sticking with it.

WORK OUT

Carefully read each of the suggestions Memma Rize would like to share with you.

1. You must want to remember.

2. You must have confidence in your ability to recall information.

3. You must try hard to remember. Don't be too easy on yourself. Don't give up quickly.

4. Be organized and neat. Organize what you know and want to recall.

5. Become very interested in what you want to remember. Give it your complete attention.

6. Practice a little at a time.

7. Practice something mentally before you do it (Mental Rehearsal).

8. Write down what you want to remember. Use a diary, lists, calendars, etc., to help you. Put your lists in a place where they will remind you of what you want to remember or carry your lists around with you. Read your lists often.

9. Try to repeat and review your notes as soon as you can. Don't be afraid to say names, dates, and places out loud.

10. Try to use mental pictures. Close your eyes and visualize.

11. Think of words and sentences to help you remember. Example: You have to learn the capital of Spain, which is Madrid. Hint: There are *bulls* in Spain. Bulls get angry or *mad*. The capital of Spain is *Mad*rid.

12. Make up flash cards and use them to help you memorize.

Side A	Side B
9×9	81

13. Highlight important information in your notes by underlining, circling, or drawing colored → arrows.

14. Put "idle" time to good use. Read over your notes while you are riding the school bus or waiting for your next class to begin. Read your notes as often as you can.

15. Make up sample tests. Take them. Correct them. Give yourself a grade. See what you already know. Spend more time learning the facts you didn't remember. Have someone else quiz you on what you have learned.

COOL DOWN

A. Select at least five of Memma Rize's suggestions that you feel will help you remember information. Write each one on a separate 3 × 5 index card. Put each suggestion to good use.

B. Choose the best memory hint from this chapter. Why do you think it will work for you?

EXERCISING YOUR MEMORY

Developing Stronger Test-Taking Skills

TEACHER INTRODUCTION

SUGGESTIONS FOR USING THIS CHAPTER

Tests are very helpful to both teachers and students, and they are a necessary part of the educational process. This chapter of the **WORKOUT** provides activities that help students develop a more positive attitude toward testing, and it offers specific suggestions for preparing for and taking tests. It will cover the following areas:

1. The Reasons for Taking Tests

2. Preparing for Tests

3. Learning How to Take Different Types of Tests (true/false, matching, multiple choice, completion, and essay)

4. Learning from Test Results

When students are in the middle grades (6-8), many teachers often assume that these students have had at least five years of testing experience and that there is no need to guide them in the test-taking process. As a result, teachers administer tests providing very little (if any) preparation for the student.

It is essential that students in the middle grades be exposed to the test-taking process. All teachers in all content areas should take class time to talk to their students about the reasons for taking tests in their particular content area and give students practice in reviewing for tests (see Chapter V and Chapter VI), taking tests, and making up their own tests. The exercises in this chapter facilitate this type of discussion and provide for some of these practice activities.

When students do poorly on tests, there are several factors that should be considered:

Factor A. The material. (Was it too difficult?)

Factor B. The test. (Did it stress the content that you emphasized as important when you were teaching the material? Or did you stress Sections 1 and 2 of the chapter in class, but then stress Sections 3 and 4 on the test? Or did all the questions deal with Section 4 when you stated that the entire chapter would be tested? Were questions worded so that students could comprehend them?)

Factor C. The student. (Was a student emotionally upset? Was a student not feeling well at the time of the test? Did a student study the wrong material? Did a student not study at all?)

Factor D. The teacher. (Did you move too quickly in an effort to cover the required curriculum? Did students need more practice with the material? Were all directions made clear?)

The following are hints which can help to make the testing process in your classroom a very worthwhile experience:

1. **Do** have clear and desirable objectives for the lesson you teach.

2. **Do** use methods and materials which will help students attain these objectives.

3. **Do** construct tests that measure the objectives of the lesson.

4. **Do** prepare questions as you teach the lesson. Jot them down during or after each class.

5. **Do** test frequently; not only at the end of a unit. Give pre-tests, section tests, and post-tests.

6. **Do** realize that a test is only one criterion by which students are evaluated. (Remember the material presented in Chapter I—**Learning Styles**.) Allow students to create a poster or an advertisement on a novel or a short story they have read. Let them create a picture or a word collage on a concept such as liberty or peace. Let them be involved in a "hands on" science project. Let them dress up as a famous composer or artist and have them tell about their music or artwork. Give them a project that relates newly learned math concepts to their daily experiences. Students who may do poorly on a test may turn in an excellent project, illustrating that they *did* gain something very valuable from the unit.

7. **Do** realize that test-making is time consuming. It requires that you not only have a good knowledge of your subject matter, but also a good knowledge of your students. Be precise in your choice of language on the test. Make every effort to construct an effective test. Create test questions which not only test factual recall but also the ability to draw conclusions and see relationships (see

Chapter IV). For more complete information on constructing an effective test, be sure to refer to a taxonomy such as Bloom's or Barrett's and an educational psychology text.

8. **Do** review tests with your students. Avoid passing tests back to students just to show them their grades. Students should be given the opportunity to see where they made their mistakes and be given the time and the opportunity to learn from their mistakes.

9. **Do** review material and repeat concepts before moving on to new material.

10. **Do** be aware of both the advantages and disadvantages of essay and objective tests.

An Essay Test
Advantages:
> allows students to express their own ideas
> allows for creativity
> allows students to organize material
> allows students to apply material they learned in the unit to other material
> is relatively easy to construct

Disadvantages:
> samples only a limited amount of material
> favors the students who can express themselves well
> is difficult and time consuming to grade

An Objective Test
Advantages:
> samples more subject matter than the essay test
> scoring is more objective
> is helpful to students who are not verbally strong

Disadvantages:
> hard to measure creative behavior
> emphasizes factual information
> often encourages guessing
> takes time to construct

11. **Do** allow your students to make up their own tests. See the Cool Down activities in this chapter on pages 80-84.

12. **Do** give students practice in taking tests. A good activity in the beginning of the school year is to prepare a test using trivia or general knowledge questions and questions relating to the class (Example: What color blazer did I wear on the first day of school?). Make sure you have a sampling of true/false, completion, matching, multiple choice, and essay. In one completion section give students choices at the bottom of the section. This technique is an excellent technique for the "slower" student. Students have fun taking these general knowledge type tests since it is a nonthreatening situation, and they gain experience in learning how to take tests. Be sure to go over the correct answers with them and offer suggestions for dealing with the different types of questions. You may want to have students work in groups of threes when they take this particular test. Students can help each other gain knowledge about the testing process.

13. Another means of giving students test-taking practice is to keep a dead-test file. A dead-test file consists of old tests that are no longer used. When students see the old tests and practice taking them, they become familiar with the teacher's testing style. Dead-test files can also help students overcome some of the anxiety commonly felt before the first big test of the year.

Although test scores are very helpful in evaluating pupils, it must be kept in mind that all types of tests have their faults, and the teacher must allow for a margin of error. Measurement and evaluation can be very helpful in determining what the student is capable of, can point out specific areas where a student needs special attention, and can encourage teachers to reflect upon their own methods and modify them (if necessary) to help students learn more efficiently.

On the whole, the testing situation is a very important part of the teaching-learning process and can be a rewarding situation if teachers take time to help their students see its value.

Developing Stronger Test-Taking Skills

STUDENT INTRODUCTION

How do you feel about tests? How would you rate tests and test-taking on a scale of 1 to 10?

Students who say that they do not like tests usually feel this way because they aren't prepared for them. They try to criticize the whole test-taking process because they are either too lazy to study or they lack the confidence and the skill to study.

Taking tests is a necessary part of your education. Your teachers use your test papers to discover if you are making progress in their classes. From a test, your teachers can see what they can do to help you learn more.

Aren't you happy when your favorite baseball team defeats its toughest opponent by a score of 10-9? Aren't dedicated golfers thrilled when they complete an 18-hole golf course with a 67 instead of a 74? Aren't members of a football team ecstatic when they win a game by two touchdowns? Isn't a talent show contestant satisfied when she scores a 29 in execution and a perfect score of 30 in the categories of originality and showmanship?

Yes, scores are a part of our society. These numbers measure talent, dedication, and progress. They show individuals their strengths and weaknesses. They spur people on to achieve more. Test results can help you, too.

This chapter of the *Study Skills Workout* will help you have a more positive attitude toward tests and offer specific suggestions for preparing for and taking tests. It will cover the following areas:

1. The Reasons for Taking Tests

2. Preparing for Tests

3. Learning How to Take Different Types of Tests

4. Learning from Test Results

By the end of this section you may even be happy that your teacher does require you to take tests!

Why Take a Test?

WARM UP

At some point in your school career you have probably wondered why you had to take a test. Why did your teachers want to make you miserable by making you learn facts and then take a test on them? Test-taking is and will be an important part of your life as a student. Learn to recognize how you can use tests to help you become a better student.

COOL DOWN

Take a clean sheet of notebook paper. Neatly copy all the true statements on the notebook paper. When you are finished, you will have eight excellent reasons why you take tests. Review them often. Believe in them.

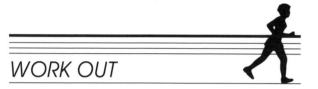

WORK OUT

Read the following statements carefully. Then, write the word **true** or **false** in front of each statement.

1. _____ Tests can give me a reason to study.

2. _____ Tests can show my teachers what I have learned.

3. _____ Teachers make tests to deliberately trap and confuse me.

4. _____ When I take a test, I have to make decisions about answers.

5. _____ Tests can teach me to budget my time.

6. _____ Tests can show my teachers that I am prepared.

7. _____ Tests can show me my mistakes.

8. _____ Teachers make tests to show me that I am stupid.

9. _____ Tests can show my teachers that I am improving.

10. _____ Tests can show my teachers if I need extra help.

Now check your answers with the answers listed on the bottom of the page.

Answers: 3 and 8 are false. The rest are true.

From *Study Skills Workout,* Copyright © 1988 Scott, Foresman and Company.

Preparing for Tests—
Push the Panic Button?

WARM UP

Fear is a normal feeling. You may be afraid of falling when you are ice skating. You may experience anxiety before you have to speak in front of a large group of people. You may get nervous when trying out for a sport, a talent competition, or a play, etc. Sometimes a little anxiety may even help you do better because you care about doing well, but **panic**—a feeling of intense fear—can make you helpless. In the following Work Out, you will discover more about eliminating that horrible feeling of panic you may experience when you take a test.

WORK OUT

Imagine you are visited by RJ-2, a "testing robot," who shows you two buttons on his side panel. One is named **PANIC,** the other **SELF-CONFIDENCE.** He wants you to press one. The choice is probably obvious, but before you decide, listen to his explanation—which he hands to you printed on his computer print-out.

COOL DOWN

Make a list of at least four reasons **why** students would panic before a test. What can these students do to prevent panic from hurting their grades? Write down your suggestions. Be prepared to share your responses with the class.

THE PANIC BUTTON

CAN HELP YOU MAKE CARELESS MISTAKES

CAN HELP YOU FORGET ANSWERS

CAN CONVINCE YOU THAT YOU CAN'T DO WELL

CAN MAKE YOU BLAME YOUR TEACHERS FOR NOT EXPLAINING THE MATERIAL

CAN MAKE YOU BLAME THE QUESTIONS FOR NOT BEING CLEAR

CAN MAKE YOU FEEL TOTALLY HELPLESS AND CONFUSED

THE SELF-CONFIDENCE BUTTON

CAN HELP YOU TO SEE TESTS AS A CHALLENGE—NOT A TORTURE SESSION

WILL MAKE YOU WANT TO SHOW YOUR TEACHERS HOW MUCH YOU HAVE LEARNED

CAN HELP YOU TO SEE A TEST AS A WAY TO SHOW YOUR TEACHERS YOU ARE PREPARED

CAN HELP YOU SEE TESTS AS A WAY TO REVIEW MATERIAL AND IMPROVE YOUR GRADES

CAN HELP YOU TO CONCENTRATE ON THE TEST QUESTIONS

CAN MAKE YOU FEEL AS IF YOU ARE IN CONTROL

How Do I Prepare?

WARM UP

Students usually feel self-confident when they have prepared for a test. If they have studied hard, they are anxious to prove to their teachers that they have learned the material. They are ready to accept the challenge that the testing situation offers. How do you gain this confidence? How do you enter a testing room saying, ''I know I've done all I possibly could do to do well on this test. I'm ready.''? The Work Out will provide you with some answers.

WORK OUT

One evening while Fiona Failure was reading the newspaper, she noticed the following ad:

Now read her reply carefully. Sylvester's suggestions are sensational:

Dear Fiona:

1. Always start to prepare for a major test at least one week before.

2. Listen carefully to what your teachers say during a review.

3. Make sure you keep a neat, well-organized notebook.

4. Review your notes carefully. Have someone quiz you on them. Make a shorter set of summary notes.

5. Review definitions, rules, formulas, and/or vocabulary words from 3 × 5 cards.

6. Review quizzes you may have had on the material you will be tested on.

7. If you still don't understand something after you review, ask your teacher or a reliable classmate to explain it to you.

8. Try to predict what questions your teacher will ask. Do you know the answers?

9. Review the **BOLDFACE** type in your book. It is a clue to important information.

10. Carefully read chapter summaries.

11. Get plenty of rest and have a good breakfast.

12. Believe in yourself. If you follow the first eleven steps, you will do well!

Best wishes,
Sylvester
Sylvester

COOL DOWN

Select five of Sylvester's suggestions that you feel are important for you. Write them on a 3x5 card titled ''Preparing for Tests.'' Read them over carefully and put them into practice before your next test. Be prepared to share the reasons why the five suggestions you selected are especially important for you.

From *Study Skills Workout*, Copyright © 1988 Scott, Foresman and Company.

Before the Test

WARM UP

You've studied very hard for your test and you feel prepared. Will this preparation guarantee your success? No. Your preparation will certainly help you, but you also must be very attentive during the time immediately before the test. In the Work Out below you will be reminded of the things you should do before you begin your test.

WORK OUT

Michele's teacher, Mrs. Dorsett, passed out a list of hints that will help Michele and her classmates do better on their tests. Maybe you can learn something from Mrs. Dorsett. Read her list carefully and be prepared to discuss these hints with your teachers and classmates.

COOL DOWN

Before you take your next test, be sure to listen very carefully to all the directions your teacher gives. It's a good habit to develop.

Hints for test-taking

1. Come prepared for your tests with the proper materials. Bring a pen, pencils, and an eraser. Don't borrow; there may be a day when no one has "extras" to give you.

2. Listen carefully to oral directions. I may tell you to skip a section, or I may even decide to give you an answer! I may tell you that you have an entire period for the test, or I may tell you that you must be finished in twenty minutes.

3. Try to look over the entire examination. Skim it over to see what I expect from you. Then you will know how much time to spend on each section.

4. Hint—Sometimes the answer to one question is partially given in another question. Keep your eyes open for these clues.

5. **RELAX.** If you've tried your best to prepare, you will pass. If you haven't studied, then you deserve to feel that sense of panic. Accept your fate and promise yourself that you will be prepared for the next test.

WARM UP

You have studied hard, listened carefully to directions, and are ready to begin your test. You're off to a good start. In the next Work Out you will receive information which will help you during the actual testing situation.

WORK OUT

When he graduated from high school, Earl Excellence was awarded a certificate for "The Student Most Likely to Succeed." His former sixth grade teacher asked him to make a speech to her present class. His topic was "How to Be a Good Student." In a portion of his speech he gave away his secrets for taking tests. As you read an excerpt of his speech, **UNDERLINE** the hints he presents.

COOL DOWN

Pretend that you are a student from the sixth grade class that Earl spoke to. Write him a thank you note. Tell him what you felt his best suggestion was. Tell him why it was a good suggestion and how it can help you. Be prepared to share your note with the class.

"When you take a test, follow the directions carefully. If they say to draw a box around the answer *and* then write the answer on the line, do both. Once I lost ten points because I misread the directions.

If you are taking a math test, write your numbers carefully in neat columns. Also, you don't want a *7* to look like a *1*. If your math teacher wants you to show your work, then show it so you won't lose points.

You must also remember to budget your time. Don't spend fifteen minutes trying to answer a question you're not sure of. The answer won't fall down from the ceiling! First, answer the questions you are sure of, then go back to the others.

When you take a test, you also have to forget about everyone else. Work on your paper. Concentrate on what you have to do; not on the raindrops hitting against the window pane or other movements in the room. I remember I used to get real nervous when someone handed in his paper ahead of mine. Later, when one of my teachers said that it didn't matter whose paper was handed in first, I relaxed a little and began to concentrate on what I had to do. Besides, if you have the time, be sure to check over your paper. Did you follow directions? Did you complete all the sections? Does your work look neat? I know teachers don't like to correct sloppy papers...."

DEVELOPING STRONGER TEST-TAKING SKILLS

Don't Forget to Fill In All the Blanks

WARM UP

Tests are usually divided into two types: objective (short answer tests) and subjective (essay tests). You will be given help on mastering both types of tests. In the Work Out below you will learn about the first type of objective test, often called "completion" or "fill in the blanks."

WORK OUT

Read the following paragraph several times. Then, cover it. Next, take the "completion" test given below.

> Sarge is a West Highland terrier. He was born on November 3, 1982. His mother's name is Lady Benton and his father's name is Lord Snowflake. Sarge has several brothers and sisters: Lady, Marco Polo, Abbey, and Sparky. Sarge is a self-important little dog who likes to show his master that he is a great watchdog. Sarge brings both love and companionship to everyone he meets.

COMPLETION

In this type of test you are recalling the information you have read and supplying this information in the blanks provided.

First, read the question carefully.

Next, fill in the blanks with the correct information. (Please remember to cover the above paragraph about Sarge when you take this test.)

1. What breed of dog is Sarge? _____
2. How many brothers and sisters does Sarge have? _____
3. When was Sarge born? _____
4. The name of Sarge's father is? _____
5. The name of Sarge's mother is? _____

Now, uncover the paper and locate the correct answers. How many did you get right? If it were a real test, how could you have prepared for it? What kind of study guide would you have made up? Be prepared to share your ideas on preparing for a test like this with the class.

COOL DOWN

Write a short paragraph or story no longer than seven sentences. Include the following words: **November 4, 2053, General Z. Taroff, the planet Zendora, the gift of friendship.** Then, make up a five-question "fill in the blanks" test. A classmate will be taking your test.

WARM UP

You have probably answered your share of true and false questions. They are a common type of **objective** test question. When you answer this type of question you are showing your teacher that you recognize a true statement from a false statement. If you know your material and read the **entire** question carefully, you will do well on true and false tests.

WORK OUT

Read the following paragraph several times. As you are reading the paragraph, try to predict some of the questions you might find on a true or false test. Then, cover the paragraph. Next, take the true or false test in the next column.

Vincent Van Gogh was a famous painter who was born on March 30, 1853 in the village of Groot Zundert. At the age of twenty-seven he began to paint in order to express his feelings for mankind. He is known for his heavy brush strokes. *Sunflowers* and *Starry Night* are two of his well-known paintings. It is hard to believe that some people used his paintings to wrap up their garbage! He died in 1890. Even though his works are world famous today, he did not receive the respect and recognition he deserved during his lifetime.

True or False
Write the word **true** or **false** in the spaces provided. Remember that a statement must be completely true to be marked true.

1. _____ Van Gogh was born on March 30, 1835.

2. _____ Van Gogh was a famous writer.

3. _____ Heavy brush strokes and deep colors can be seen in Van Gogh's paintings.

4. _____ Van Gogh was very well-respected at the time of his death.

5. _____ The painting *Starry Night* was painted by Van Gogh.

Now, uncover the paragraph and locate the correct answers to the questions. Check your answers. How many did you get right? If this were a real test, how could you have prepared for it?

COOL DOWN

Select one of the following topics. Next, do a little background reading in an encyclopedia to make yourself familiar with the facts about your topic. Then, make up a five-question true or false test. Be sure that you can correctly answer your own test.

dogs—plants—minerals—oceans—trees—insects

A Multiple Choice

WARM UP

Another type of **objective** test is the multiple choice test. In this type of test you have to recognize important information that you have learned. When you take a multiple choice test, it is important to eliminate the choices that you are sure are incorrect. Then, look at the remaining choices and decide on the best answer.

WORK OUT

From your everyday knowledge answer the multiple choice questions below. First, read the question carefully. Next, examine all of your choices. Then, select the answer and write the correct capital letter in the space provided.

COOL DOWN

Make up a five-question multiple choice test about your favorite things. Then, have a friend or family member answer it.

EXAMPLE: My favorite season is
A. fall   B. winter
C. summer   D. spring

Be sure you make it clear in the directions that they are to answer these questions about you, not about themselves. After they have completed the test, be sure to give them the correct answers. See if they know you as well as they thought they did. If they answered some questions incorrectly, go over the reasons for the correct answers. This discussion after the test will give you an opportunity to share some interesting aspects of your personality with someone you feel close to.

Multiple Choice

1. _____ The capital of the United States is

   A. Atlanta   B. Philadelphia   C. Washington, D.C.   D. Moscow

2. _____ An animal you would find on a dairy farm in Pennsylvania is

   A. an armadillo   B. a cow   C. a lion   D. a panda bear

3. _____ A diamond is

   A. an animal   B. a vegetable   C. a mineral   D. none of these

4. _____ John F. Kennedy was the _____ President of the United States.

   A. 2nd   B. 20th   C. 48th   D. 35th

5. _____ There are _____ states in the United States.

   A. 49   B. 48   C. 56   D. none of these

Answers: 1-C, 2-B, 3-C, 4-D, 5-D

WARM UP

The fourth type of **objective** test that you will learn about in this chapter is the matching test. In this type of test, you show your teacher that you recognize information that you learned by correctly matching up two terms or facts. In this type of test it is always very helpful to read the directions carefully. It is also a good idea to match the terms that you are sure of first.

WORK OUT

Take the following matching tests. Use a reference book if you have to.

Matching Test   Test 1

For each word in Column A match the proper word from Column B. Use the capital letter for your answer. A single letter may be used more than once. Remember, whenever you take a matching test be sure to preview the items you will be working with by quickly reading the information in both columns. Begin the test by reading the first item in Column A. Then, read all of your choices in Column B. (Don't ''jump'' at the first answer you think is correct; there may be a better answer farther down the list.) Complete all the matches you are sure of first. Then, go back to the ones you experienced difficulty with.

Column A

1. _____ North America
2. _____ Albany
3. _____ San Jose
4. _____ Europe
5. _____ Spain
6. _____ Houston

Column B

A. state
B. city
C. country
D. continent

Matching Test   Test 2

For each state in Column A match the proper nickname from Column B. Use the capital letter for your answer. Don't forget to look at the helpful hints listed on this page.

Column A

1. _____ Massachusetts
2. _____ Texas
3. _____ Florida
4. _____ California
5. _____ Kentucky
6. _____ Tennessee
7. _____ Michigan

Column B

A. The Keystone State
B. The Bay State
C. The Wolverine State
D. The Bluegrass State
E. The Golden State
F. The Peninsula State
G. The Big Ben State
H. The Lone Star State
I. The Beehive State

Answers:
Test 1 1-D, 2-B, 3-B, 4-D, 5-C, 6-B.
Test 2 1-B, 2-H, 3-F, 4-E, 5-D, 6-G, 7-C.
Pennsylvania—The Keystone State; Utah—The Beehive State.

COOL DOWN

Select a chapter from your science book or social studies book (or other text that your teacher recommends) and make up a ten-question matching test. Close your book. Take the test. Then, correct it. What have you learned from doing this particular exercise? How can it help you in the future?

DEVELOPING STRONGER TEST-TAKING SKILLS

An Effective Essay (Part I)

WARM UP

Now that you have become familiar with four types of **objective** tests (fill-in-the-blanks or completion, true or false, multiple choice, and matching), make an effort to learn how to answer a subjective type test—the essay question. Some students get very nervous when they see an essay test because there are no answers to choose from or blanks to fill in. But if you see an essay question as a chance to really show your teachers how well you have prepared for their tests, there's really no reason to panic. In the next two Work Outs you will have the opportunity to learn how to effectively answer an essay question.

WORK OUT

Elena loves essay questions, and she always seems to do very well when she answers them. When her teacher completed a study skills unit with Elena's class, Elena volunteered to make a poster listing important things to remember when you take an essay test.

Read her poster over very carefully. Her ideas could help you.

A TEN POINT PLAN TO MASTER THE ESSAY QUESTION
BY ELENA DIMIDIAN

1. Read the question carefully.
   (Don't answer a question that wasn't asked.)

2. Turn the question into a statement.

3. In the margin or on a piece of scrap paper, jot down as many facts as you can to include in your answer.

4. Organize your information. Number the important points as you list them.

5. Begin writing your response.

6. Be sure to include examples to back up your statements and to give definitions for the terms you mention.

7. Express your ideas clearly. Don't ramble on and on.

8. Make sure your answer is neatly written so your teacher will **not** have trouble reading it.

9. Write an ending. Either summarize the points you have made or restate your topic (opening) sentence.

10. If you have time, check over your answer to make sure it makes sense. Check your punctuation and spelling.

COOL DOWN

When your teachers give you an essay question, they usually want you to do one of the following:

1. **describe**—give particular details; how it looked; what it was like—Describe a summer day.

2. **explain**—give reasons for something; account for situations—Explain why the Civil War ended.

3. **discuss**—look at different points of view; give both sides—Discuss tax reform.

4. **identify**—list and make associations; name and give details—Identify three of El Greco's paintings.

5. **compare**—point out how things are alike as well as how they are different—Compare love and hate.

6. **contrast**—point out only differences—Contrast dogs and cats.

Become familiar with these terms. Select one of the terms listed above and then make up an essay question that uses the term in it. Be prepared to answer your own essay question.

An Effective Essay (Part II)

WARM UP

When you answer an essay question you not only have to recall the information you have learned, but also you must organize it effectively and express it clearly. An essay question is a subjective type test because your teacher can be more personal when grading your papers. Your teacher may only take off a few points because you only identified four reasons for a war breaking out instead of the five you were expected to list. You also may be rewarded with a few extra points if you organized your ideas very effectively.

WORK OUT

Mr. Penkala gave the following essay question to his reading class:

DISCUSS THE THREE GHOSTS OR SPIRITS IN THE CHARLES DICKENS CLASSIC, *A CHRISTMAS CAROL.* EXPLAIN THE EFFECT THEY HAD ON SCROOGE.

Examine the three sample responses three of the students wrote on the next page. See if you can explain why Mr. Penkala gave them the grades he did. Don't be afraid to get some help from Elena's chart on page 83. Be prepared to share your reasons with the class.

COOL DOWN

Take your reading or social studies book (or any other text that your teacher suggests) and find a section you enjoy. Make up an essay question and then answer it. Be sure to check the essay terms defined in **AN EFFECTIVE ESSAY— PART I.** Be prepared to share your question and response with the class.

Student #1

The ghosts came to Scrooge on Christmas Eve to show that he had to change his ways.

Grade F

Student #2

Ebenezer Scrooge was a stingy old man who was not kind to Tiny Tim. He hated Christmas. His partner was Jacob Marley. Marley visited Scrooge. Marley sent three ghosts. The ghosts took Scrooge to different places and showed him different things. When Scrooge woke up, he wanted to see if he missed Christmas. He changed.

Grade D

Student #3

In *A Christmas Carol* Charles Dickens introduces us to three ghosts or spirits: 1) the Spirit of Christmas Past, 2) the Spirit of Christmas Present, and 3) the Spirit of Christmas Yet to Come. In my answer I will describe the work of each spirit and the effect that each spirit's visit had on Ebenezer Scrooge.

The Ghost of Christmas Past seemed to be a combination of a child and an old person. This spirit took Mr. Scrooge back to scenes when he was younger. The spirit showed him how happy he used to be and that his love of money began to change things.

The Ghost of Christmas Present was a jolly giant who wore a long robe. This ghost showed Scrooge how other people, including his worker Bob Cratchit, were spending Christmas. He also showed Scrooge how some very poor people had to live.

The last of the spirits—the Ghost of Christmas Yet to Come—was a scary figure who showed Scrooge how unhappy the future would be. Tiny Tim would die, and no one would be sad about Scrooge's death. This spirit really frightened Ebenezer, and he was ready to be a new person. He wanted to change the terrible things the spirits showed him about his future.

These three spirits were all important in *A Christmas Carol*. They helped Scrooge to see that he could change his ways and be a happy man who cared about Christmas and other people.

Grade A

When the Test Is Over

WARM UP

When you receive your test results, you may have a variety of reactions. A test score may make you extremely proud or very disappointed. A grade might leave you feeling sorry that your score wasn't higher or pleased that you passed the test. An important fact to remember is that a low grade doesn't mean you are a bad person. It means that on a particular test you did not do well. You can improve.

WORK OUT

Hopeful Harold did poorly on his math test, but he was not discouraged. He realized that there was nothing he could do to change the grade. He also realized that he could work harder the next time. When his teacher returned the tests, Harold looked over his mistakes and realized where his problems were. He made a list of his trouble spots.

1. He made three mistakes with the nine times tables.

2. He read a word problem wrong. Instead of dividing 5 into 48, he divided 5 into 84.

3. He didn't know the four definitions for the math terms that his teacher wanted him to define on the test. Later, he discovered they were given a week ago Friday—a day he was absent.

Give Harold some ideas on how he can avoid making mistakes like these on his next test.

Problem #1 Hints

_____

_____

_____

Problem #2 Hints

_____

_____

_____

Problem #3 Hints

_____

_____

_____

COOL DOWN

A. When you get back your next test, identify the areas that you did well in and the areas that caused you problems.

Example:

Weak points—I didn't include enough information in my essay answer.

Strong points—I did very well on a difficult true and false section.

B. Carefully read the following test-taking resolutions. Mentally rehearse them.

TEST-TAKING RESOLUTIONS: A NEW OUTLOOK

Resolution #1. I will believe that tests can help me to become a better student.

Resolution #2. I will listen carefully in class so I can tell what my teacher feels is important.

Resolution #3. I will take neat and complete notes.

Resolution #4. I will start my review early.

Resolution #5. I will come to a testing situation prepared with the proper materials.

Resolution #6. I will listen very carefully as my teacher gives directions to the test.

Resolution #7. I will read the test directions and test questions very carefully.

Resolution #8. I will know my test material well enough so I will be prepared for any type of test my teacher gives. I will be able to handle fill-in-the-blanks, true or false, multiple choice, and matching tests (objective). I will be able to master the essay test (subjective), too.

Resolution #9. I will look over my tests carefully when they are returned to me. I will discover where I went wrong.

Resolution #10. I will learn from my mistakes and try to do better the next time.

Record Your Grades

WARM UP

Make a copy of or detach the next page from your workbook. Carry it with you at all times during school. (Keep it in a safe place so you don't lose it. Try to glue or fasten it to the inside of a sturdy notebook cover.)

COOL DOWN

Use the grids on the next page to keep a record of your grades. Remember to write your actual grades in the column before you graph the number. Use a separate grid for each subject.

WORK OUT

Directions: The actual grades are in the column on the left side. Graph the grades on the grid paper below.

EXAMPLE:

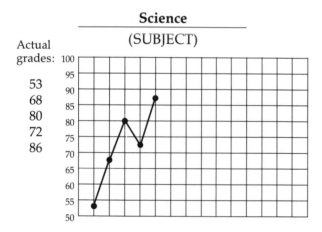

Graph the following grades:

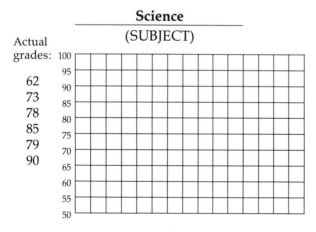

DEVELOPING STRONGER TEST-TAKING SKILLS

Appendix

CHARTING YOUR PROGRESS

This section will show you how to record your grades. You will also see how much progress you have made in developing your study skills.

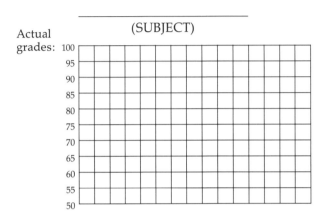

Actual grades:

(SUBJECT)

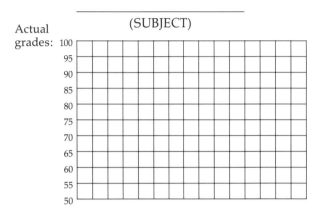

Actual grades:

(SUBJECT)

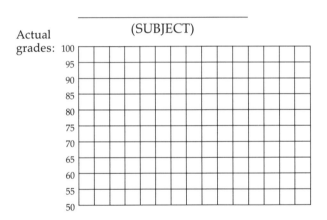

Actual grades:

(SUBJECT)

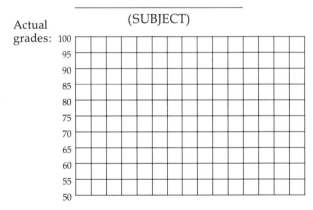

Actual grades:

(SUBJECT)

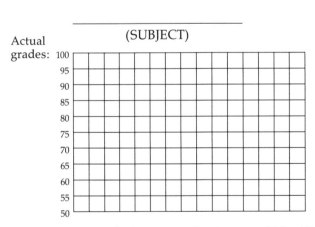

Actual grades:

(SUBJECT)

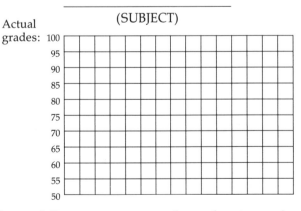

Actual grades:

(SUBJECT)

Keeping a record of your grades is a good idea! It's fun to follow your progress throughout a marking period.